DAILY
WISDOM
ON OUR
SPIRITUAL
FATHER

St. Joseph
Gems

Donald H. Calloway, MIC

Available from:
Marian Helpers Center
Stockbridge, MA 01263

Prayerline: 1-800-804-3823
Orderline: 1-800-462-7426
Websites: fathercalloway.com
marian.org

Publication Date:
February 1, 2018

Imprimi Potest:
Very Rev. Kazimierz Chwalek, MIC
Provincial Superior
The Blessed Virgin Mary, Mother of Mercy Province
January 1, 2018

Acknowledgments: Mr. and Mrs. Donald & LaChita Calloway;
Matthew Calloway; Ileana E. Salazar, MA; Teresa de Jesus Macias;
Bethany Price; Theresa Vonderschmitt; Milanka Lachman, LCHS

ISBN: 9781596144200
Library of Congress Control Number: 2017960092

Design by Kathy Szpak
Editing and Proofreading: Chris Sparks

Cover image: *San José, Refugio de los Agonizantes*, Miguel Cabrera (1695-1768)
© Museo Nacional del Virreinato, Secretaría de Cultura, INAH
Tepozotlán, México

Printed in the United States of America

MARIAN PRESS
STOCKBRIDGE · MA 01263

2019

Dedication

To my father,
Donald R. Calloway,
a man so much like St. Joseph.

Was he [St. Joseph] old or young? Most of the statues and pictures we see of Joseph today represent him as an old man with a gray beard, one who took Mary and her vow under his protection with somewhat the same detachment as a doctor would pick up a baby girl in a nursery. We have, of course, no historical evidence whatsoever concerning the age of Joseph. Some apocryphal accounts picture him as an old man; Fathers of the Church, after the fourth century, followed this legend rather rigidly ...

But when one searches for the reasons why Christian art should have pictured Joseph as aged, we discover that it was in order better to safeguard the virginity of Mary. Somehow, the assumption had crept in that senility was a better protector of virginity than adolescence. Art thus unconsciously made Joseph a spouse chaste and pure by age rather than by virtue. But this is like assuming that the best way to show that a man would never steal is to picture him without hands ...

But more than that, to make Joseph out as old portrays for us a man who had little vital energy left, rather than one who, having it, kept it in chains for God's sake and for his holy purposes. To make Joseph appear pure only because his flesh had aged is like glorifying a mountain stream that has dried. The Church will not ordain a man to his priesthood who has not his vital powers. She wants men who have something to tame, rather than those who are tame because they have no energy to be wild. It should be no different with God.

— *Venerable Fulton J. Sheen*

REFUGIO DE LOS AGONIZANTES

DO YOU LOVE ST. JOSEPH? I can tell you with absolute certainty that Jesus and Mary do. Jesus loves him because St. Joseph faithfully served as his virginal father on earth. As his earthly, adoptive father, St. Joseph modeled all the virtues for his divine Son, teaching the Incarnate God how to be a man and make sacrifices. Jesus looked up to St. Joseph (see Lk 2:51-52). In fact, it was St. Joseph who saved Jesus by taking him to Egypt when Herod wanted to murder the newborn King. It is for this reason that St. Joseph is the only human person who has been given the title of "savior of the Savior." Saint Joseph truly is the man closest to Christ. Even in eternity, Jesus perpetually shines his divine face on St. Joseph and responds to his every request and desire.

The Virgin Mary loves St. Joseph because he was her faithful, chaste, and virtuous husband. Saint Joseph treated his bride's heart, soul, and body as a sacred shrine, set aside for the Lord and his purposes. Mary's feminine heart always felt safe and secure in the strength, holiness, and calmness of her beloved St. Joseph. Along with his virginal bride, the first to bring the Messiah to the nations, St. Joseph is the second greatest human person in history because he, too, shared in the role of bringing Jesus to souls.

Many have often wondered, "If St. Joseph is so great, why are there no words from him recorded in the New Testament?" Perhaps the answer is found in the Old Testament wisdom literature, where we read the following: "He who has understanding spares his words, and a man of understanding is of a calm spirit" (Prov 17:27). In a certain sense, the greatest statement that the inspired word of God could make about St. Joseph is the fact that God's Son Himself desired to call St. Joseph his father. What more could be said? Everything else that could be stated about the virginal father of Jesus would appear as a mere footnote in comparison.

Yet, while the New Testament doesn't recount any of St. Joseph's words, saints and popes throughout history have been inspired by the Holy Spirit to speak for him, and to praise the greatness of St. Joseph. In the early centuries of the Church, scholarly men such as St. Augustine, St. Jerome, St. John Chrysostom, and St. John Damascene delighted in preaching about the greatness of the virginal father of Jesus. During the medieval and early modern period, St. Teresa of Avila, St. Francis de Sales, and St. Bernardine of Siena extolled the virtues of St. Joseph and implored all Christians to turn to him in filial supplication. In more modern times, Blessed William Joseph Chaminade, St. Joseph Marello, St. Peter

Julian Eymard, St. Luigi Guanella, St. Josemaria Escriva, and St. Andre Bessette have all given tremendous testimony to the importance of having a devotion to St. Joseph.

Nonetheless, I believe that within the last century and a half, Heaven has clearly called us to increase our knowledge of and devotion to St. Joseph. One only has to consider the many significant events connected with St. Joseph that have taken place in the last 150 years to recognize this movement of the Holy Spirit:

1868 – Blessed Jean-Joseph Lataste, OP, writes a letter to Blessed Pope Pius IX asking him to declare St. Joseph the "Universal Patron of the Church."

1870 – Blessed Pope Pius IX declares St. Joseph the "Universal Patron of the Church."

1871 – Founding of the Josephites by Cardinal Herbert A. Vaughan

1878 – Founding of the Oblates of St. Joseph by St. Joseph Marello

1879 – Apparitions at Knock, Ireland. Saint Joseph appears with the Blessed Virgin Mary, St. John the Apostle, and Jesus (appearing as the Lamb of God).

1889 – Pope Leo XIII writes *Quamquam Pluries*, an encyclical letter on St. Joseph.

1904 – Saint Andre Bessette constructs an oratory dedicated to St. Joseph in Montreal, Canada. It expands, is declared a minor basilica, and finally is completed in 1967. Today, it is known as St. Joseph's Oratory and is considered by many to be the preeminent international center of devotion to St. Joseph.

1908 – Saint Luigi Guanella begins constructing a church dedicated to St. Joseph in Rome. It is completed and consecrated as a basilica in 1912.

1914 – Saint Luigi Guanella founds the Pious Union of St. Joseph for the Salvation of the Dying.

1917 – Apparitions at Fatima, Portugal. During the last apparition on October 13, St. Joseph appears holding the Child Jesus and blessing the world.

1921 – Pope Benedict XV inserts the phrase "Blessed be St. Joseph, her most chaste spouse" into the Divine Praises.

1947 – Spanish Discalced Carmelites found *Estudios Josefinos*, the first theological journal devoted to St. Joseph.

1950s – The alleged apparitions of Our Lady of America given to Sr. Mary Ephrem greatly emphasize a renewed devotion to St. Joseph, and St. Joseph himself speaks to the visionary about this devotion.

1955 – Venerable Pope Pius XII establishes the Feast of St. Joseph the Worker, to be celebrated on May 1.

1962 – Saint Pope John XXIII inserts St. Joseph's name into the Canon of the Mass (Eucharistic Prayer I).

1989 – Saint Pope John Paul II writes *Redemptoris Custos*, an encyclical letter on St. Joseph.

2013 – Pope Francis, echoing and fulfilling the intentions of Pope Emeritus Benedict XVI, inserts the name of St. Joseph into all Eucharistic Prayers. He also consecrates Vatican City State to St. Joseph.

The Holy Spirit is definitely seeking to bring St. Joseph to our attention. In the past, saints have often lamented that St. Joseph is the "forgotten person of the earthly trinity," referring to the tradition of understanding the Holy Family as an icon of the Trinity in Heaven. Saint Joseph is the earthly icon of God the Father; Jesus is the true Son of God; and the Blessed Virgin Mary is the icon of the Holy Spirit. It is true that St. Joseph is well known as the patron of a happy death, since he died in the arms of Jesus and Mary, but he is much more than that. He is our spiritual father! As such, he desires to lead us to Jesus, Mary, the Church, and growth in virtue.

During a time of great famine in the Old Testament, Pharaoh instructed the Egyptians to do the following to save themselves from starving: "*Ite ad Ioseph et quidquid vobis dixerit facite*," that is, "Go to Joseph and do all that he shall say to you" (Gen 41:55). The patriarch Joseph was in charge of all the granaries in Egypt, which was known at that time as the bread basket of the world. In the New Testament, we have the new patriarch Joseph ("patriarch" means "father"); he was the one chosen to bring the true bread of Heaven out of Egypt and feed the entire world. Through the New Testament bread basket of the world, that is, the Catholic Church, the Holy Spirit is speaking to people today and telling them, "*Ite ad Ioseph!* Go to Joseph!"

That's the purpose of this book. Like the other books I have put together (*Marian Gems: Daily Wisdom on Our Lady* and *Rosary Gems: Daily Wisdom on the Holy Rosary* [see page 252], this book offers a way of knowing more about St. Joseph by giving you a daily quote about him from a saint, blessed, or pope. By coming to know more about St. Joseph, we can come to love him more and learn to turn to him more frequently in our spiritual lives.

We need St. Joseph today. I pray this book helps you come to know and love St. Joseph, your spiritual father, more and more. Use this book to ask for his intercession, especially by praying the Litany of St. Joseph (see page 211). Also, ask for the communion of saints to help you grow in your love for St. Joseph! Pray the prayer provided after each quote, asking a different saint each day to help you grow in your love for St. Joseph.

Ite ad Ioseph!

Very Rev. Donald H. Calloway, MIC, STL
Vicar Provincial — Marian Fathers of the Immaculate Conception
Blessed Virgin Mary, Mother of Mercy Province

JANUARY

January 1

Inspired by the Gospel, the Fathers of the Church from the earliest centuries stressed that just as St. Joseph took loving care of Mary and gladly dedicated himself to Jesus Christ's upbringing, he likewise watches over and protects Christ's Mystical Body, that is, the Church, of which the Virgin Mary is the exemplar and model.

– St. John Paul II

Mary, Mother of God, pray for us!

January 2

The Almighty has concentrated in St. Joseph, as in a Sun of unrivalled lustre, the combined light and splendor of all the other saints.

– St. Gregory of Nazianzen

St. Gregory of Nazianzen, pray for us!

15

January 3

Who, I ask, will deny that while Joseph held
Christ in his arms as a father and spoke
to him as a father ... he [Jesus] impressed
ineffable joys upon him!

— ST. BERNARDINE OF SIENA

St. Elizabeth Ann Seton, pray for us!

January 4

In Joseph ... heads of the household are
blessed with the unsurpassed model
of fatherly watchfulness and care.

— POPE LEO XIII

St. Manuel González García, pray for us!

January 5

Let us trust in God and St. Joseph.

– ST. JOHN NEUMANN

St. John Neumann, pray for us!

January 6

I have only my great devotion to
St. Joseph. This it is that guides me
and gives me full confidence.

– ST. ANDRÉ BESSETTE

St. André Bessette, pray for us!

January 7

What could Jesus Christ refuse St. Joseph
who never refused him anything
during his mortal life on earth?

– ST. AUGUSTINE

Blessed Edward Waterson, pray for us!

January 8

In him [St. Joseph] are enshrined the worth
of bishops, the generosity of martyrs,
and of all the other saints.

— St. Francis de Sales

Blessed Gabriele Allegra, pray for us!

January 9

I do not remember ever having asked for
any grace that he [St. Joseph]
has not obtained for me.

— St. Teresa of Avila

Blessed Tommaso Reggio, pray for us!

January 10

Together with Mary, Joseph is the first
guardian of this divine mystery
[the Incarnation].

– ST. JOHN PAUL II

Blessed Anna of the Angels Monteagudo, pray for us!

January 11

He [St. Joseph] is head of the Holy Family,
father of the trinity on earth which resembles
so closely the Holy Trinity on high.

– ST. PETER JULIAN EYMARD

Blessed William Carter, pray for us!

January 12

The Catholic Church rightly honors with its highest
cultus [honor] and venerates with a feeling of deep reverence
the illustrious patriarch blessed Joseph, now crowned
with glory and honor in heaven, whom Almighty God,
in preference to all his saints, willed on earth to be the
chaste and true spouse of the Immaculate Virgin Mary
as well as the putative father of his only-begotten Son.

– BLESSED POPE PIUS IX

St. Marguerite Bourgeoys, pray for us!

January 13

Joseph carried Jesus Christ first to Egypt, then to Judea,
and so traced for us the path of the apostles who preached
his name to the Jews and to the Gentiles.

– ST. HILARY OF POITIERS

St. Hilary of Poitiers, pray for us!

January 14

If you wish to be close to Christ,
we again today repeat, "Go to Joseph."

– VENERABLE POPE PIUS XII

Blessed Marie-Anne Vaillot, pray for us!

January 15

As he himself [Jesus] was subject to St. Joseph
while on earth, recognizing in him the authority
of foster father and guardian, so now in heaven
he is pleased to grant all his requests.

– ST. TERESA OF AVILA

St. Francisco Fernández de Capillas, pray for us!

January 16

This holy man [St. Joseph] had such towering
dignity and glory that the Eternal Father
most generously bestowed on him a likeness
of his own primacy over his Son incarnate.

— St. Bernardine of Siena

St. Joseph Vaz, pray for us!

January 17

O chaste spouse of the most pure and most holy of creatures,
how happy you must be for having found such favor and
grace before the Eternal Father, who gave his Son;
before the Son who made you the tutor of his sacred
humanity; before the Holy Spirit who entrusted his
spouse to you so that you could be like the cherubim
who guarded the fruit of life in the garden of Eden.

— Blessed William Joseph Chaminade

St. Marianne Cope, pray for us!

January 18

Jesus' obedience to his mother and legal father fulfills the fourth commandment perfectly and was the temporal image of his filial obedience to his Father in heaven.

– CATECHISM OF THE CATHOLIC CHURCH

Blessed Gregory Khomyshyn, pray for us!

January 19

Who can conceive St. Joseph's feelings on
hearing himself called "father"
by the child Jesus?

– ST. BERNARDINE OF SIENA

Blessed Monique Pichery, pray for us!

January 20

We wonder why the Gospel makes so little
mention of St. Joseph. But did it not say
everything when it taught us that
he was the husband of Mary?

— BLESSED WILLIAM JOSEPH CHAMINADE

St. Tommaso of Cori, pray for us!

January 21

Although you [St. Joseph] are not necessary for
the [child's] conception and birth, nevertheless
you will be necessary for [his] sustenance;
and your first care will concern his name.

— ST. ALBERT THE GREAT

St. Gianna Beretta Molla, pray for us!

January 22

Mary is the depository of all graces,
but who can better induce her to open the celestial
treasury than Joseph, her glorious spouse?

– BLESSED WILLIAM JOSEPH CHAMINADE

Blessed William Joseph Chaminade, pray for us!

January 23

Saint Joseph, may you and your immaculate
spouse assist me in the final struggle.

– ST. JOHN NEUMANN

Blessed Edward Stransham, pray for us!

January 24

Glorious St. Joseph, spouse of the Virgin Mary,
we beseech you through the heart of Jesus Christ,
grant to us your fatherly protection.

— ST. FRANCIS DE SALES

St. Francis de Sales, pray for us!

January 25

Joseph, of royal blood, united by marriage
to the greatest and holiest of women,
reputed the father of the Son of God,
passed his life in labor, and won by the toil
of the artisan the needful support of his family.

— POPE LEO XIII

Blessed Marie Cassin, pray for us!

January 26

In our time Our Lady has helped us comprehend
and love her dear and chaste husband, St. Joseph.
She has told us of the mystery surrounding him and
of his greatness. She has let us know something of
her love for St. Joseph, that most lovable saint who
for years held the Word made flesh in his arms.

— BLESSED GABRIELE ALLEGRA

Blessed Gabriele Allegra, pray for us!

January 27

Would that I could persuade all men to foster devotion
to this glorious saint [Joseph] because of the singular proof
that I have of the many favors he obtains for us of God.

— ST. TERESA OF AVILA

Blessed George Matulaitis, pray for us!

January 28

According to [St.] Jerome and Origen, Joseph had no suspicion of adultery because he knew the modesty and chastity of Mary. Moreover, he had read in Scripture that the virgin would conceive and that "a shoot shall sprout from the stock of Jesse, and from his roots a bud shall blossom." He knew also that Mary was descended from the line of David. Thus it was easier for him to believe that Isaiah's prophecy had been accomplished in her than to think that she could have let herself descend into debauchery. This is why, considering himself unworthy to live with a person of such great sanctity, he wanted to send her away secretly — like when Peter says to Jesus, "Depart from me, Lord, for I am a sinful man!"

– ST. THOMAS AQUINAS

St. Thomas Aquinas, pray for us!

January 29

Saint Joseph desired nothing, wanted nothing that was not for the greater glory of God.

– ST. JOSEPH MARELLO

Blessed Michał Kozal, pray for us!

January 30

If it is true that the Blessed Virgin is the keeper of all heavenly graces, that her love for the elect is the source of their glory and happiness, what must be the glory of St. Joseph whom she was obliged to love above all the saints, just as a good wife must love her husband above all men. Meditate on this.

– BLESSED WILLIAM JOSEPH CHAMINADE

Blessed Boleslava Lament, pray for us!

January 31

There are many saints to whom God has given the power to assist us in the necessities of life, but the power given to St. Joseph is unlimited: It extends to all our needs, and all those who invoke him with confidence are sure to be heard.

– ST. THOMAS AQUINAS

St. John Bosco, pray for us!

FEBRUARY

February 1

When the little Jesus was growing big, and was wearied with much walking on the journeys they made, how Joseph, full of compassion, made him rest in his bosom!

– St. Bernardine of Siena

St. Sabás Reyes Salazar, pray for us!

February 2

O most faithful saint who shared the mysteries of our redemption, glorious St. Joseph, the prophecy of Simeon regarding the sufferings of Jesus and Mary caused thee to shudder with mortal dread, but at the same time filled thee with a blessed joy for the salvation and glorious resurrection which, he foretold, would be attained by countless souls.

– Blessed Januarius Maria Sarnelli

St. Donald of Ogilvy, pray for us!

31

February 3

Let us ask St. Joseph to foster
staunch vocations for our Lord.

– ST. PETER JULIAN EYMARD

Blessed Anne-Marie Rivier, pray for us!

February 4

Jesus and Mary themselves obey and offer
their homage to Joseph, for they reverence what
the hand of God has established in him, namely,
the authority of spouse and the authority of father.

– POPE PIUS XI

St. Joan of Valois, pray for us!

February 5

Saint Joseph, as you have all learned at home and at school,
was a very holy man. He had to be, because he was
married to the Virgin Mary, the purest, the holiest,
the most exalted of all God's creatures.

– VENERABLE POPE PIUS XII

Blessed Elizabeth Canori Mora, pray for us!

February 6

Whereas Adam and Eve were the source of evil which was
unleashed on the world, Joseph and Mary are the summit
from which holiness spreads all over the earth.

– ST. JOHN PAUL II

Blessed Rosalie Rendu, pray for us!

February 7

Go to Joseph! Have recourse with special confidence
to St. Joseph, for his protection is most powerful,
as he is the patron of the universal Church.

– BLESSED POPE PIUS IX

Blessed Pope Pius IX, pray for us!

February 8

He [St. Joseph] belongs to the working-class,
and he bore the burdens of poverty
for himself and the Holy Family,
whose tender and vigilant head he was.

– POPE PIUS XI

St. Josephine Bakhita, pray for us!

February 9

I believe that this man, St. Joseph, was adorned with the
most pure virginity, the most profound humility,
the most ardent love and charity towards God.

– St. Bernardine of Siena

Blessed Anne Catherine Emmerich, pray for us!

February 10

Knowing by experience St. Joseph's astonishing influence
with God, I would wish to persuade everyone to honor
him with particular devotion. I have always seen those who
honored him in a special manner make progress in virtue,
for this heavenly protector favors in a striking manner
the spiritual advancement of souls who
commend themselves to him.

– St. Teresa of Avila

St. José Luis Sánchez del Río, pray for us!

February 11

How many times did he [St. Joseph], like the lone sparrow,
nestle on the roof of that holy temple of the Divinity,
contemplating this divine Child sleeping in his arms,
and thinking of his eternal repose in
the bosom of the heavenly Father?

— Blessed William Joseph Chaminade

Our Lady of Lourdes, pray for us!

February 12

O inestimable tribute to Mary! Joseph believed in
her chastity more than in her womb, in grace more
than in nature! He plainly saw the conception,
and he was incapable of suspecting fornication.
He believed that it was more possible for a woman to
conceive without a man than for Mary to be able to sin.

— St. John Chrysostom

St. José Luis Sánchez del Río, pray for us!

February 13

O with what sweetness he [St. Joseph]
heard the lisping child call him father!

– St. Bernardine of Siena

St. Catherine de Ricci, pray for us!

February 14

Truly, I doubt not that the angels, wondering and adoring,
came thronging in countless multitudes to that poor
workshop to admire the humility of him who guarded
that dear and divine Child, and labored at his
carpenter's trade to support the Son and
the Mother who were committed to his care.

– St. Francis de Sales

Blessed Vicente Vilar David, pray for us!

February 15

Joseph's rest revealed God's will to him.

– POPE FRANCIS

Blessed Michael Sopocko, pray for us!

February 16

Saint Joseph was called by God to serve
the person and mission of Jesus directly
through the exercise of his fatherhood.

– ST. JOHN PAUL II

Blessed Giuseppe Allamano, pray for us!

February 17

He [St. Joseph] always favors with especial protection those souls who are enrolled beneath the standard of Mary!

– St. Mary Magdalen de Pazzi

St. Alexis Falconieri, pray for us!

February 18

You don't have to wait to be old or lifeless to practice the virtue of chastity. Purity comes from love; and the strength and gaiety of youth are no obstacle for noble love. Joseph had a young heart and a young body when he married Mary, when he learned of the mystery of her divine motherhood, when he lived in her company, respecting the integrity God wished to give the world as one more sign that he had come to share the life of his creatures. Anyone who cannot understand a love like that knows very little of true love and is a complete stranger to the Christian meaning of chastity.

– St. Josemaria Escriva

St. Geltrude Comensoli, pray for us!

February 19

Joseph was deeply pious; he prayed much
for the coming of the Messiah.

– BLESSED ANNE CATHERINE EMMERICH

St. Francisco Marto, pray for us!

February 20

As Christians, you too are called,
like Joseph, to make a home for Jesus.

– POPE FRANCIS

St. Jacinta Marto, pray for us!

February 21

It is perfectly in accordance with the faith and spirit of the
Church, to honor as a virgin not only the Mother of God,
but likewise Joseph, his [Jesus'] reputed father,
and the guardian of his infancy.

– St. Peter Damian

St. Peter Damian, pray for us!

February 22

Mary belonged to Joseph, and Joseph to Mary, so much
so that their marriage was very real, since they gave themselves to each other. But how could they do this? Behold the
triumph of purity. They reciprocally gave their virginity,
and over this virginity they gave each other a mutual right.
What right? To safeguard the other's virtue.

– St. Peter Julian Eymard

Blessed Stefan Wincenty Frelichowski, pray for us!

February 23

What prudence was required to educate
a God become a child, who willed to obey
him [St. Joseph] for thirty years!

– BLESSED WILLIAM JOSEPH CHAMINADE

Blessed Josephine Vannini, pray for us!

February 24

Be in good spirits under the fatherly mantle
of St. Joseph, a place of safest refuge
in trials and tribulations.

– ST. JOSEPH MARELLO

Blessed Tommaso Maria Fusco, pray for us!

February 25

There is no doubt that St. Joseph, to whom the Mother
of the Savior was espoused, was a good and faithful man.
A faithful and prudent servant, I say, whom the Lord
appointed to be the consolation of his mother,
the tutor of his own person, and the one faithful
coadjutor on earth of his great counsel.

– St. Bernard of Clairvaux

Blessed Maria Ludovica de Angelis, pray for us!

February 26

By that assistance which Jesus and Mary gave thee
[St. Joseph] at death, I beg thee to protect me in a special
way at the hour of my death, so that dying assisted by thee,
in the company of Jesus and Mary, I may go to thank
thee in heaven, and in thy company to sing
God's praises for all eternity.

– St. Alphonsus Liguori

Blessed Jacques-Désiré Laval, pray for us!

February 27

By means of [his] espousal [to Mary],
Joseph's testimony proved the
Christ was born of a virgin.

— ST. THOMAS AQUINAS

Blessed Maria Caridad Brader, pray for us!

February 28

God gave him [St. Joseph] to Mary as
companion of her purity. For that reason he
had to surpass all the saints, and even the
angels and the cherubim.

— ST. PETER JULIAN EYMARD

Blessed Villana de'Botti, pray for us!

February 29

Why did he [St. Joseph] wish to leave her [Mary]? Listen, now, no longer to my opinion, but to that of the Fathers [of the Church]. The reason why Joseph wished to leave Mary is that same for which Peter distances himself from the Lord by saying, *Depart from me, Lord, for I am a sinner* [Lk 5:8]; this is also the reason why the centurion left his home while saying: *Lord, I am not worthy that you should come under my roof* [Mt 8:8]. And so, Joseph, considering himself unworthy and a sinner, said to himself that such a great person, whose marvelous and superior dignity he admired, could not deign to live together with him.

– St. Bernard of Clairvaux

St. Philomena, pray for us!

MARCH

March 1

We earnestly exhort all the bishops of the Catholic
world that in the Church's present need they should
induce the faithful to implore more earnestly
the powerful intercession of St. Joseph.

– POPE BENEDICT XV

St. José Gabriel del Rosario Brochero, pray for us!

March 2

Joseph is the one whom God chose to be the "overseer of
the Lord's birth," the one who has the responsibility to look
after the Son of God's "ordained" entry into the world,
in accordance with divine dispositions and human laws.

– ST. JOHN PAUL II

St. Angela of the Cross, pray for us!

March 3

Saint Joseph was an ordinary sort of man on whom God relied to do great things. He did exactly what the Lord wanted him to do, in each and every event that went to make up his life. That is why Scripture praises Joseph as "a just man." And in Hebrew a just man means a good and faithful servant of God, someone who fulfills the divine will, or who is honorable and charitable toward his neighbor.

– St. Josemaria Escriva

St. Katherine Drexel, pray for us!

March 4

I will say what seems to me to be correct as it did to the Fathers before me. The reason for Mary's espousal was the reason for Thomas' doubt. Just as Thomas by doubting and handling Christ became the most irrefutable witness of the Lord's resurrection, so was Joseph an irrefutable witness to Mary's chastity by becoming her spouse and by carefully approving her mode of life during the time she was in his custody.

– St. Bernard of Clairvaux

Blessed Matthias Araki, pray for us!

March 5

I take refuge in thy arms [St. Joseph],
so that thou mayest lead me in the path of virtue,
and assist me at the hour of my death.

– St. Clement Mary Hofbauer

Blessed Dionysius Fugishima, pray for us!

March 6

Jesus wished to become indebted to St. Joseph for the
necessities of life, and of this holy patriarch alone it
may be said that he saved the life of his Savior.

– St. Madaleine Sophie Barat

St. Atilano Cruz Alvarado, pray for us!

March 7

I promise to honor thee [St. Joseph]
every day by some special act of devotion and
by placing myself under thy daily protection.

– St. Alphonsus Liguori

Blessed John Larke, pray for us!

March 8

May he [St. Joseph] always guard,
protect and enlighten families.

– St. John Paul II

St. Siméon-François Berneux, pray for us!

March 9

Nothing will be refused him [St. Joseph],
neither by Our Lady nor by his glorious Son.

— St. Francis de Sales

St. Dominic Savio, pray for us!

March 10

Since God has wanted to obey you [St. Joseph],
allow me to be in your service, to honor you
and love you as my Lord and Master.

— St. Alphonsus Liguori

St. John Ogilvie, pray for us!

March 11

Let us love Jesus above all, let us love Mary as our mother;
but then, how could we keep from loving Joseph, who was
so intimately united to both Jesus and Mary? And how
can we honor him better than by imitating his virtues?
Now, what else did he do in all his life but contemplate,
study, and adore Jesus, even in the midst of his daily labors?
Behold, therefore, our model.

– St. Madaleine Sophie Barat

St. Mateo Correa, pray for us!

March 12

It was necessary that divine Providence should
commit her [Mary] to the charge and
guardianship of a man absolutely pure.

– St. Francis de Sales

St. Luigi Orione, pray for us!

March 13

It is truly a grace for the soul to make the acquaintance of the holy patriarch [St. Joseph] of the New Testament.

– BLESSED GABRIELE ALLEGRA

Blessed Bedřich Bachstein, pray for us!

March 14

Just as he [St. Joseph] was virginally the husband, so he was virginally the father.

– ST. AUGUSTINE

Blessed Giacomo Cusmano, pray for us!

March 15

Saint Joseph, my loving father, I place myself forever under thy protection; look on me as thy child, and keep me from all sin.

– ST. CLEMENT MARY HOFBAUER

St. Clement Mary Hofbauer, pray for us!

March 16

Joseph obeyed the explicit command of the angel
and took Mary into his home, while respecting
the fact that she belonged exclusively to God.

– ST. JOHN PAUL II

St. Louise de Marillac, pray for us!

March 17

As Almighty God appointed Joseph, son of the
patriarch Jacob, over all the land of Egypt to save grain
for the people, so when the fullness of time was come and
he was about to send on earth his only-begotten Son,
the Savior of the world, he chose another Joseph of whom
he made the lord and chief of his household and possessions,
the guardian of his choicest treasures.

– BLESSED POPE PIUS IX

St. John Sarkander, pray for us!

March 18

Since St. Joseph was a just man, holy and perfect in all virtues, it is certain that nothing that savored of impurity ever entered his life, and since there is nothing on record that he ever had any other spouse than the Virgin Mary, it is also certain that he remained a virgin all his life.

– St. Jerome

St. Richard Pampuri, pray for us!

March 19

For several years I have asked some particular favor on his [St. Joseph's] feast day and have never been disappointed. If on account of some imperfection my request did not have God's glory in view, he always obtained for me something else instead which was more important.

– St. Teresa of Avila

St. Joseph, pray for us!

March 20

No one can describe the adoration of this [St. Joseph's] noble soul. He saw nothing, yet he believed; his faith had to pierce the virginal veil of Mary. So likewise with you! Under the veil of the Sacred Species your faith must see our Lord. Ask St. Joseph for his lively, constant faith.

— ST. PETER JULIAN EYMARD

St. Jozef Bilczewski, pray for us!

March 21

The gospel accounts understand the virginal conception of Jesus as a divine work that surpasses all human understanding and possibility. "That which is conceived in her [Mary] is of the Holy Spirit," said the angel to Joseph about Mary his fiancée.

— CATECHISM OF THE CATHOLIC CHURCH

Blessed Maria Candida of the Eucharist, pray for us!

March 22

Who can ever understand how great he [St. Joseph]
had to be in this virtue of virginity who was
destined by the Eternal Father to be the guardian,
or rather the companion, of Mary's virginity?

– ST. FRANCIS DE SALES

St. Nicholas Owen, pray for us!

March 23

As the Church's Liturgy teaches, he [St. Joseph]
"cooperated in the fullness of time in the great mystery
of salvation" and is truly a "minister of salvation."

– ST. JOHN PAUL II

Blessed Clemens August Graf von Galen, pray for us!

March 24

When we receive Holy Communion,
let us consider that Jesus comes to us as a little baby,
and then let us pray that St. Joseph help[s] us
welcome him, as when he held him in his arms.

– ST. JOSEPH MARELLO

Blessed Alberto Marvelli, pray for us!

March 25

Looking at the gospel texts of both Matthew and Luke,
one can also say that Joseph is the first to share in the faith
of the Mother of God, and that in doing so he supports
his spouse in the faith of the divine annunciation.

– ST. JOHN PAUL II

Blessed Omelyan Kovch, pray for us!

March 26

Joseph saves Mary's reputation, the lineage of Jesus,
the integrity of the Child, his rootedness in the land of
Israel ... Joseph is also saved from an isolated life, from a life
that would have been perhaps less turbulent, but that would
have lacked the consolation of carrying God in his arms.

– POPE FRANCIS

Blessed Magdalena Caterina Morano, pray for us!

March 27

Joseph, knowing Mary's chastity and wondering
at what had occurred, concealed in silence
the mystery he did not fathom.

– ST. JEROME

St. Jenaro Sánchez Delgadillo, pray for us!

March 28

How holy he [St. Joseph] must have been!
Under his fatherly protection and ceaseless, tireless
care the young boy [Jesus] grew into manhood.

— VENERABLE POPE PIUS XII

Blessed Bartolomé Blanco Márquez, pray for us!

March 29

Through his complete self-sacrifice, Joseph
expressed his generous love for the Mother of God,
and gave her a husband's "gift of self."

— ST. JOHN PAUL II

Blessed Jerzy Popiełuszko, pray for us!

March 30

Joseph's faith does not falter,
he obeys quickly and to the letter.

– St. Josemaria Escriva

St. Leonard Murialdo, pray for us!

March 31

When Joseph was dying, Mary sat at the head of his bed,
holding him in her arms. Jesus stood just below her near
Joseph's breast. The whole room was brilliant with light
and full of angels. After his death, his hands were crossed
on his breast, he was wrapped from head to foot in a white
winding sheet, laid in a narrow casket, and placed in
a very beautiful tomb, the gift of a good man.

– Blessed Anne Catherine Emmerich

St. Román Adame Rosales, pray for us!

APRIL

April 1

To give life to someone is the greatest of all gifts.
To save a life is the next. Who gave life to Jesus? It
was Mary. Who saved his life? It was Joseph. Ask St.
Paul who persecuted him. Saint Peter who denied him.
Ask all the saints who put him to death. But if we ask,
"Who saved his life?" Be silent, patriarchs, be silent,
prophets, be silent, apostles, confessors and martyrs.
Let St. Joseph speak, for this honor is his alone;
he alone is the savior of his Savior.

– BLESSED WILLIAM JOSEPH CHAMINADE

Blessed Anacleto González Flores, pray for us!

April 2

The growth of Jesus "in wisdom and in stature, and in favor with God and man" (Lk 2:52) took place within the Holy Family under the eyes of Joseph, who had the important task of "raising" Jesus, that is, feeding, clothing and educating him in the Law and in a trade, in keeping with the duties of a father.

– St. John Paul II

St. Pedro Calungsod, pray for us!

April 3

Joseph also was virginal through Mary in order that from a virginal marriage a virginal son might be born.

– St. Jerome

St. Hermann Joseph, pray for us!

April 4

I have great love for St. Joseph, because he is a man of silence and strength. On my table, I have an image of St. Joseph sleeping. Even when he is asleep, he is taking care of the Church! Yes! We know that he can do that. So when I have a problem, a difficulty, I write a little note and I put it underneath St. Joseph, so that he can dream about it! In other words, I tell him: "Pray for this problem!"

– POPE FRANCIS

St. Gaetano Catanoso, pray for us!

April 5

The Eternal Father confided to the care of St. Joseph his own only-begotten Son.

– VENERABLE POPE PIUS XII

St. Vincent Ferrer, pray for us!

April 6

Make him [St. Joseph] the patron of your
family and you will soon have tangible
proof of his protecting hand.

– ST. PETER JULIAN EYMARD

Blessed Pierina Morosini, pray for us!

April 7

Intercede for us [St. Joseph] with your foster Son, Jesus;
obtain for us the favor and protection of your
beloved spouse, the Blessed Virgin Mary.

– ST. BERNARDINE OF SIENA

Blessed Domingo Iturrate Zubero, pray for us!

April 8

Jesus must have resembled Joseph: in his way of working,
in the features of his character, in his way of speaking.
Jesus' realism, his eye for detail, the way he sat at table
and broke bread, his preference for using everyday
situations to give doctrine — all this reflects his
childhood and the influence of Joseph.

– St. Josemaria Escriva

St. Julia Billiart, pray for us!

April 9

Joseph was the special protector of the Virgin
and also of the Savior in his infancy.

– St. Thomas Aquinas

St. Euphrasia Eluvathingal, pray for us!

April 10

Do you not know that the Son of God preferred the purity
of the flesh to such an extent that he became man in the
closed womb of a virgin rather than in the respectability of
marriage? And if it does not suffice for you that not only the
mother is a virgin, there remains the belief of the Church
that he who served as father [St. Joseph] is also a virgin.

— St. Peter Damian

Blessed Anthony Neyrot, pray for us!

April 11

With a love that transformed him,
he [St. Joseph] was drawn to Jesus, as to his
dearest son presented him by the
Holy Spirit in his virginal wife.

— St. Bernardine of Siena

St. Gemma Galgani, pray for us!

April 12

He [St. Joseph] was not a passive instrument
in the great work of our salvation; he played a
very active role, and that is why he was included
in the merciful counsels of the incarnate Wisdom.

– BLESSED WILLIAM JOSEPH CHAMINADE

St. Agustín Caloca Cortés, pray for us!

April 13

We should more efficaciously implore the
compassion of God through the merits
and intercession of St. Joseph.

– BLESSED POPE PIUS IX

St. Pope Martin I, pray for us!

April 14

Imitate St. Joseph: Defend Jesus, the Holy Church,
and the Pope, according to your abilities.

— ST. MAXIMILIAN KOLBE

St. Peter González, pray for us!

April 15

Joseph was of such exalted nobility that in a
certain fashion, if I may so speak, he gave temporal
nobility to God in the Lord Jesus Christ.

— ST. BERNARDINE OF SIENA

Blessed Maria Troncatti, pray for us!

April 16

If anyone cannot find a master to teach him how
to pray, let him take this glorious saint [Joseph]
as his master, and he will not go astray.

– ST. BERNADETTE SOUBIROUS

St. Bernadette Soubirous, pray for us!

April 17

Poor St. Joseph! He had to submit to death and
leave behind him Jesus and Mary: Jesus to be crucified
and abandoned by his people; Mary, to suffer alone,
unassisted. How his love for them was crucified!

– ST. PETER JULIAN EYMARD

St. Benedict Joseph Labre, pray for us!

April 18

Since we all must die, we should cherish a special
devotion to St. Joseph that he may
obtain for us a happy death.

– ST. ALPHONSUS LIGUORI

Blessed Marie-Anne Blondin, pray for us!

April 19

He [St. Joseph] is patron of vocations, so pray to him for the
grace of fulfilling your duties well and of directing your
children in their path of life. Inspire them with devotion
to St. Joseph. It will bring them happiness.

– ST. PETER JULIAN EYMARD

Blessed James Duckett, pray for us!

April 20

Saint Joseph did not do extraordinary things,
but rather by the constant practice of the ordinary
and common virtues, he attained that sanctity
which elevates him above all the other saints.

— ST. JOSEPH MARELLO

St. Agnes of Montepulciano, pray for us!

April 21

My dear St. Joseph, pray to Jesus for me. Certainly he
can never refuse thee anything, since he obeyed all thy
orders while on earth. Ask him to detach me from all
creatures and from myself, to inflame me with his holy
love, and then to do with me what he pleases.

— ST. ALPHONSUS LIGUORI

St. Lorenzo Ruiz, pray for us!

April 22

Oh, how happy shall we be if we can merit a share
in his [St. Joseph's] holy intercession!

— ST. FRANCIS DE SALES

Blessed Maria Gabriella Sagheddu, pray for us!

April 23

Virgins can look to him [St. Joseph] for their
pattern and as the guardian of virginal integrity.

— POPE LEO XIII

St. Augustin Schoeffler, pray for us!

April 24

The former Joseph [of the Old Testament] was holy,
righteous, pious, chaste; but this Joseph so far surpasses him
in holiness and perfection as the sun outshines the moon.

— ST. LAWRENCE OF BRINDISI

St. Benedetto Menni, pray for us!

April 25

All of the so-called "private" or "hidden" life
of Jesus is entrusted to Joseph's guardianship.

– St. John Paul II

Blessed Robert Anderton, pray for us!

April 26

All for Jesus, all for Mary, all in imitation of thee,
O patriarch Joseph! Such will be my desire in life
and at the hour of my death. Amen.

– Blessed Hyacinth Marie Cormier

Blessed Rolando Rivi, pray for us!

April 27

Joseph is called Mary's husband. By his solicitude, he was like a father; by his espousal, he was like a husband; by his protection of chastity, he was the guide of virginity. What sort of ordinance of Divine Wisdom would choose an unclean witness and protector for the virgin mother?

– St. Albert the Great

St. Lawrence Huong, pray for us!

April 28

Hail Joseph the just, wisdom is with you;
blessed are you among all men and blessed is Jesus,
the fruit of Mary, your faithful spouse.

– St. Louis de Montfort

St. Louis de Montfort, pray for us!

April 29

If Joseph was so engaged, heart and soul, in protecting
and providing for that little family at Nazareth, don't you
think that now in heaven he is the same loving father
and guardian of the whole Church, of all its members,
as he was of its Head on earth?

– VENERABLE POPE PIUS XII

St. Catherine of Siena, pray for us!

April 30

This flower of Israel [St. Joseph] had the faith of Abraham,
the piety of David his ancestor, the wisdom of the prophets,
a patience more heroic than that of Job and of Tobias, and a
zeal greater than that of Elijah for the glory of God.

– BLESSED GABRIELE ALLEGRA

St. Pope Pius V, pray for us!

MAY

May 1

In this month of May, I would like to recall the importance
and beauty of the prayer of the Holy Rosary. Reciting the
Hail Mary, we are led to contemplate the mysteries of Jesus,
that is, to reflect on the key moments of his life, so that,
as with Mary and St Joseph, he is the center of our
thoughts, of our attention and our actions.

– POPE FRANCIS

St. Joseph the Worker, pray for us!

May 2

Joseph, the just man, is appointed to be the steward of
the mysteries of God, the *paterfamilias* and guardian of the
sanctuary, which is Mary the bride and the Logos in her.
He [Joseph] thus becomes the icon of the bishop,
to whom the bride is betrothed; she is not at his
disposal but under his protection.

– POPE BENEDICT XVI

St. José María Rubio, pray for us!

May 3

No husband and wife ever loved one
another so much as Joseph and Mary.

– VENERABLE FULTON J. SHEEN

Blessed Marie-Léonie Paradis, pray for us!

May 4

For just as Mary is called the mother of John
[see Jn 19:26-27] because of love and not because
she gave him birth, so Joseph is called the father of
Christ, not by reason of generation, but by reason of
the care he expended in supporting and rearing him.

– ST. CYRIL OF JERUSALEM

Blessed Ceferino Giménez Malla, pray for us!

May 5

The humble workman of Nazareth not only personifies before God and the Church the dignity of the man who works with his hands, but he is always the provident guardian of you and of your families.

– VENERABLE POPE PIUS XII

Blessed Edmund Rice, pray for us!

May 6

He [St. Joseph] who merited to be called the father of the Lord remained virginal with her [Mary].

– ST. JEROME

Blessed Anna Rosa Gattorno, pray for us!

May 7

Saint Joseph foresaw Mary's tears and misery.
He would have desired to stay by her side, and he
must have begged Jesus to be allowed to remain on
earth that he might climb Calvary and sustain Mary.

— St. Peter Julian Eymard

St. Rose Venerini, pray for us!

May 8

I do not know how one can meditate on the care
which the Blessed Virgin took of the Divine Child,
without thanking St. Joseph for the care he likewise
took of both the mother and the Child.

— St. Teresa of Avila

St. Magdalene of Canossa, pray for us!

May 9

Why did he [St. Joseph] wish to leave her [Mary]? He saw, with sacred astonishment, that she bore a special quality of the divine presence and while not being able to understand this mystery, he wished to leave her.

– St. Bernard of Clairvaux

Blessed Karolina Gerhardinger, pray for us!

May 10

Joseph wanted to give the Virgin her liberty, not because he suspected her of adultery, but [because] out of respect for her sanctity he feared to live together with her.

– St. Thomas Aquinas

St. Damien of Molokai, pray for us!

May 11

To you, O Blessed Joseph, we come in our trials,
and having asked the help of your most holy spouse,
we confidently ask for your patronage.

– POPE LEO XIII

Blessed Ivan Merz, pray for us!

May 12

Mary belonged to him [St. Joseph],
and was planted close to him, like a glorious palm
by the side of its beloved palm tree.

– ST. FRANCIS DE SALES

St. Leopold Mandić, pray for us!

May 13

Since Mary is what might be called a "virginizer" of young men as well as women, and the greatest inspiration of Christian purity, should she not logically have begun by inspiring and virginizing the first youth whom she had probably ever met — Joseph, the Just? It was not by diminishing his power to love but by elevating it that she would have her first conquest, and in her own spouse, the man who was a man, and not a senile watchman!

– VENERABLE FULTON J. SHEEN

Our Lady of Fatima, pray for us!

May 14

If God gave Joseph as a spouse to the Virgin, he assuredly gave him not only as a companion in life, a witness of her virginity, and the guardian of her honor, but also as a sharer in her exalted dignity by reason of the conjugal tie itself.

– POPE LEO XIII

St. Maria Mazzarello, pray for us!

May 15

Saint Joseph sweetly and continuously stimulates
us to love, serve, and imitate the Queen of his heart,
the Immaculate Mother of Jesus.

— BLESSED GABRIELE ALLEGRA

St. Isidore, pray for us!

May 16

O glorious patriarch St. Joseph, humble and just workman
of Nazareth, who has given to all Christians but especially
to us [Catholic workers], the example of a perfect life of
assiduous work and admirable union with Mary and Jesus,
help us in our daily tasks, so that we Catholic workmen
may also be able to find in them the efficacious means
to glorify our Lord, to sanctify ourselves, and to be
useful to the society in which we live.

— VENERABLE POPE PIUS XII

St. Simon Stock, pray for us!

May 17

God would not have given the most holy Virgin to Joseph as his wife unless he had been holy and righteous. What right-minded father would ever give his most beloved daughter in marriage to a man who was not moral and beyond reproach according to his rank and state in life?

– St. Lawrence of Brindisi

Blessed Antonia Mesina, pray for us!

May 18

The Virgin [Mary] has been wed to the virginal bridegroom [Joseph]. Yet she — who married Joseph out of obedience to her elders — has no fear for her virginity under Joseph's protection. Having placed her trust in God, she delegated to a man the safeguarding of the greatest treasure. She — who had dedicated the flower of virginity to God earlier in a solemn ceremony — had no doubt that she would have a virginal spouse.

– St. Stanislaus Papczynski

St. Stanislaus Papczynski, pray for us!

May 19

Both Mary and Joseph had made a vow to remain virgins all
the days of their lives; and God wished them to be united in
the bonds of marriage, not because they repented of the vow
already made, but to be confirmed in it and to encourage
each other to continue in this holy relation.

— ST. FRANCIS DE SALES

Blessed Franz Jägerstätter, pray for us!

May 20

The dignity and glory of St. Joseph is such that the
Eternal Father conferred upon him with greatest liberality,
a likeness to his own supremacy over his incarnate Son.

— ST. BERNARDINE OF SIENA

St. Bernardine of Siena, pray for us!

May 21

O glorious St. Joseph, model of all who labor, obtain for me the grace to work in the spirit of penance in expiation for my numberless sins; preferring devotion to duty to my inclinations; to work with joy and gratitude, regarding it as an honor to develop and employ by work the gifts which I have received from God; to work with order, peace, patience, and moderation, without ever recoiling before weariness and difficulties; to work, especially, with a pure intention and detached from myself, ever having death before my eyes and the account which I must give for time lost, for talents unused, for good omitted, and for vain satisfaction in success, so fatal to the work of God.

– BLESSED HYACINTH MARIE CORMIER

Blessed Hyacinth Marie Cormier, pray for us!

May 22

Keep from us, O most loving father [St. Joseph], all blight of error and corruption.

– POPE LEO XIII

St. Rita of Cascia, pray for us!

May 23

What a dignity to be the guardian of our Lord,
and not only that, but to be even his reputed father,
to be the husband of his most holy Mother!

— St. Francis de Sales

St. Cristóbal Magallanes Jara, pray for us!

May 24

I have never known a person to have been truly devoted to
St. Joseph and to have rendered him special honor without
seeing him advance rapidly in virtue; because the holy
patriarch assists with special care those who recommend
themselves to him ... should the reader not believe my
words, I only ask him for the love of God to make a trial
and he will experience for himself what a grace it is to
recommend oneself to this glorious patriarch.

— St. Teresa of Avila

Blessed Louis-Zéphirin Moreau, pray for us!

May 25

The two greatest personages who ever lived on this earth subjected themselves to him [St. Joseph].

– St. Madaleine Sophie Barat

St. Madaleine Sophie Barat, pray for us!

May 26

How great a share had not the glorious St. Joseph in the chalice of Jesus' passion, by the services which he rendered to his sacred humanity!

– St. Mary Magdalen de Pazzi

St. Mary Magdalen de Pazzi, pray for us!

May 27

How thou [St. Joseph] didst rejoice to have always near you God himself, and to see the idols of the Egyptians fall prostrate to the ground before him.

– Blessed Januarius Maria Sarnelli

St. Eugène de Mazenod, pray for us!

May 28

He [St. Joseph] guarded from death the Child
threatened by a monarch's jealousy,
and found for him a refuge.

— POPE LEO XIII

St. David Galván Bermúdez, pray for us!

May 29

If the lily, by being exposed only for a few days to
the light and heat of the sun, acquires its dazzling
whiteness, who can conceive the extraordinary
degree of purity to which St. Joseph was exalted,
by being exposed as he was day and night for so
many years to the rays of the Sun of Justice, and of
the Mystical Moon who derives all her
splendor from him [Jesus]?

— ST. FRANCIS DE SALES

Blessed Joseph Gérard, pray for us!

May 30

If St. Joseph did not grant us favors,
he would no longer be St. Joseph.

– St. Joseph Marello

St. Joseph Marello, pray for us!

May 31

Devotion to St. Joseph is something very precious
for Christian mothers because St. Joseph
is patron of Christian families.

– St. Peter Julian Eymard

St. Miguel de la Mora, pray for us!

JUNE

June 1

O Blessed Joseph, be ever mindful of us;
give us the benefit of your powerful prayers.

— St. Bernardine of Siena

Blessed Teofilius Matulionis, pray for us!

June 2

Those who invoke him [St. Joseph], shall obtain from God,
by his intercession, the gift of chastity, and shall not be
conquered by the temptations of the senses.

— Venerable Mary of Agreda

St. Luis Bátiz Sainz, pray for us!

June 3

To Joseph of Nazareth, a simple workman, our heavenly Father entrusted his most precious treasures to guard, protect, and support.

— BLESSED GABRIELE ALLEGRA

Blessed Giuseppe Oddi, pray for us!

June 4

Since it is written that God "will do the will of them that fear him," how can he refuse to do the will of St. Joseph who nourished him for so long with the sweat of his brow?

— ST. AMBROSE

St. Filippo Smaldone, pray for us!

June 5

He [St. Joseph] is the proof that in order to be a good and genuine follower of Christ, there is no need of great things — it is enough to have the common, simple, and human virtues, but they need to be true and authentic.

– BLESSED POPE PAUL VI

Blessed Maria Karlowska, pray for us!

June 6

God has granted to the other saints only the grace to help in this or that particular need, but I know from experience that the glorious St. Joseph extends his power to all our necessities. This is our Lord's way of giving us to understand that, as he was subject to him during his mortal life on earth by recognizing his authority as foster father, he is now pleased to do his will in heaven by hearing and granting all his requests.

– ST. TERESA OF AVILA

St. Bonifacia Rodríguez Castro, pray for us!

June 7

All Christians belong to Joseph because
Jesus and Mary belonged to him.

– ST. LEONARD OF PORT MAURICE

St. Anthony Mary Gianelli, pray for us!

June 8

I choose thee [St. Joseph] after Mary to
be my chief advocate and protector.

– ST. ALPHONSUS LIGUORI

St. Jacques Berthieu, pray for us!

June 9

No one will ever be able worthily to praise Joseph, whom thou, O true only-begotten Son of the Eternal Father, has designed to have for thy foster father!

– ST. EPHREM THE SYRIAN

St. Ephrem the Syrian, pray for us!

June 10

If it is true, as we are bound to believe, that in virtue of the Blessed Sacrament which we receive, our bodies will come to life again in the day of judgment (Jn 6:55), how could we doubt that our Lord raised up to heaven, in body and soul, the glorious St. Joseph? For he had the honor and the grace of carrying him so often in his blessed arms, those arms in which our Lord took so much pleasure.

– ST. FRANCIS DE SALES

Blessed Caspar Sadamatsu, pray for us!

June 11

Pharaoh, the mighty king of Egypt, exalted Joseph and made him the highest prince in his kingdom, because he stored up the grain and bread and saved the people of his entire kingdom. So Joseph saved and protected Christ, who is the living bread and gives eternal life to the world.

– St. Lawrence of Brindisi

St. Paula Frassinetti, pray for us!

June 12

Although he [St. Joseph] never adored our Lord under the Eucharistic species and never had the happiness of communicating [receiving Holy Communion], he did possess and adore Jesus in human form.

– St. Peter Julian Eymard

*Blessed Anthony Leszczewicz and
Blessed George Kaszyra, pray for us!*

June 13

Let us ask St. Joseph to be
our spiritual director.

– St. Joseph Marello

St. Gaspar Bertoni, pray for us!

June 14

Let him who cannot find anyone to teach him to pray,
choose this glorious saint [Joseph] for his master, and
he will not stray from the right path.

– St. Teresa of Avila

Blessed Michael Tozo, pray for us!

June 15

Among humans, the effect of living together is that we usually end up by having a very mediocre love for each other because, as relationships are kept up, we become more and more aware of each other's shortcomings. On the contrary, as St. Joseph continued to live with Jesus, he constantly grew in admiration for his holiness. We can thereby understand what burning love he managed to have for him, having lived in this intimacy, which defies description.

– St. Alphonsus Liguori

St. Emily de Vialar, pray for us!

June 16

Noble St. Joseph, I rejoice that God found you worthy of holding this eminent position whereby, established as the father of Jesus, you saw the one whose orders heaven and earth obey subjecting himself to your authority.

– St. Alphonsus Liguori

St. Jean-François Régis, pray for us!

June 17

Though not his father by generation, he [St. Joseph] was his father in his upbringing, his care, and the affection of his heart. It seems to me, therefore, that Joseph is clearly that holiest of all the saints, holier than the patriarchs, than the prophets, than the apostles, than all the other saints. The objection cannot be raised that the Lord said of John the Baptist: *Among those born of women there has been none greater than John the Baptist* [Lk 7:28; see also Mt 11:11]. Just as this cannot be understood to mean that John is even holier than Christ or the Blessed Virgin, so it can't be understood in reference to blessed Joseph, the spouse of the Virgin Mary and the father of Christ, for just as husband and wife are one flesh, so too Joseph and Mary were one heart, one soul, one spirit. And as in that first marriage God created Eve to be like Adam, so in this second marriage he made Joseph to be like the Blessed Virgin in holiness and justice.

– St. Lawrence of Brindisi

St. Albert Chmielowski, pray for us!

June 18

If all the faithful are debtors to the Virgin Mother for being made worthy through her to receive the Redeemer, there can be no doubt that next to the Mother of God we owe to St. Joseph our special homage and veneration.

— St. Bernardine of Siena

St. Elisabeth of Schönau, pray for us!

June 19

Although St. Joseph was not the real father of Jesus, yet because he was the real husband of Mary, there existed between the two such a noble relationship that Jesus dutifully called him father and was subject to him in the natural order. It is this heavenly alliance that constitutes St. Joseph the special patriarch of Christians and more especially the patriarch and the head of priests, who are the true members of the mystical body of Jesus.

— Blessed William Joseph Chaminade

St. Juliana Falconieri, pray for us!

June 20

[Saint] Joseph is still charged with
guarding the Living Bread!

– Venerable Fulton J. Sheen

Blessed Conor O'Devany, pray for us!

June 21

We must be convinced that, in consideration of his great
merits, God will not refuse St. Joseph any grace
he asks for those who honor him.

– St. Alphonsus Liguori

Blessed John Kinsako, pray for us!

June 22

Saint Joseph was the first adorer, the first religious.

– St. Peter Julian Eymard

Sts. Thomas More and John Fisher, pray for us!

June 23

This was a unique and magnificent mission [given to St. Joseph], that of protecting the Son of God and King of the world; the mission of protecting the virginity and holiness of Mary; the singular mission of entering into participation in the great mystery hidden from the eyes of past ages, and of thus cooperating in the Incarnation and in the Redemption.

– POPE PIUS XI

St. Joseph Cafasso, pray for us!

June 24

The Virgin Mary, accordingly, is the holiest of all the saints and angels, because she is closest to Christ. After Mary, who is closer to Christ than Joseph? She is his mother, but he is his father. Though not his natural father, Joseph still was his legal father.

– ST. LAWRENCE OF BRINDISI

St. María Guadalupe García Zavala, pray for us!

June 25

Grant that according to your example [St. Joseph]
we may keep our eyes fixed on our mother Mary,
your most sweet spouse, who silently used to do her
weaving in a corner of your modest workshop, with
the sweetest smile playing on her lips.

– VENERABLE POPE PIUS XII

Blessed Paul Shinsuki, pray for us!

June 26

He [St. Joseph] did exactly what our Lord
wanted him to do, in each and every event
that went to make up his life.

– ST. JOSEMARÍA ESCRIVÁ

St. Josemaría Escrivá, pray for us!

June 27

We must pray to St. Joseph, but always and in everything will nothing but what God wills.

— ST. ANDRÉ BESSETTE

St. André Bessette, pray for us!

June 28

He [St. Joseph] employed himself joyfully in the education of Jesus Christ.

— ST. IRENAEUS OF LYONS

St. Irenaeus of Lyons, pray for us!

June 29

The holy example of Jesus Christ who, while upon earth, honored St. Joseph so highly and was obedient to him during his life should be sufficient to inflame the hearts of all with devotion to this saint.

– St. Alphonsus Liguori

Sts. Peter and Paul, pray for us!

June 30

O most watchful Guardian of the Incarnate Son of God, glorious St. Joseph, what toil was thine in supporting and waiting upon the Son of the most high God, especially in the flight into Egypt!

– Blessed Januarius Maria Sarnelli

Blessed Januarius Maria Sarnelli, pray for us!

JULY

July 1

How great is the dignity of that son of David,
Joseph, the husband of Mary!

— Blessed Gabriele Allegra

Blessed Ignatius Falzon, pray for us!

July 2

What many kings and prophets desired to see, and saw
not; desired to hear, and heard not; he [St. Joseph] was
allowed not merely to hear and see, but also to carry,
lead, embrace, kiss, nourish, and protect.

— St. Bernard of Clairvaux

St. Junipero Serra, pray for us!

July 3

At the workbench where he [St. Joseph] plied his trade together with Jesus, Joseph brought human work closer to the mystery of the Redemption.

– St. John Paul II

Blessed Eugénie Joubert, pray for us!

July 4

Saint Joseph is the model of those humble ones that Christianity raises up to great destinies.

– Blessed Pope Paul VI

Blessed Pier Giorgio Frassati, pray for us!

July 5

He [St. Joseph] is the father of Christians,
since he is the depository of the seed of
grace which begot Christians.

– BLESSED WILLIAM JOSEPH CHAMINADE

St. Anthony Maria Zaccaria, pray for us!

July 6

He [St. Joseph] set himself to protect with a mighty love
and a daily solicitude his spouse and the Divine Infant;
regularly by his work he earned what was necessary for the
one and the other for nourishment and clothing.

– POPE LEO XIII

St. Maria Goretti, pray for us!

July 7

He [St. Joseph] is not only a confessor, but he is more than a confessor, and has a dignity greater than that of all the saints, greater even than that of the angels.

– ST. FRANCIS DE SALES

Blessed Maria Romero Meneses, pray for us!

July 8

From the same fact that the most holy Virgin is the mother of Jesus Christ is she the mother of all Christians whom she bore on Mount Calvary amid the supreme throes of the Redemption: Jesus Christ is, in a manner, the first-born of Christians, who by the adoption and Redemption are his brothers. And for such reasons the Blessed Patriarch [St. Joseph] looks upon the multitude of Christians who make up the Church as confided especially to his trust.

– POPE LEO XIII

Blessed Nazaria Ignacia Mesa, pray for us!

July 9

God wills that he [St. Joseph] should be always poor, which is one of the heaviest trials that he can lay upon him, and he submits lovingly not for a time only, but for his whole life. And what poverty — despised, rejected, needy poverty!

– St. Francis de Sales

St. Veronica Giuliani, pray for us!

July 10

To him was entrusted the Divine Child
when Herod loosed his assassins against him.

– Pope Pius XI

Blessed Emmanuel Ruiz, pray for us!

July 11

It is natural and worthy that as the Blessed Joseph
ministered to all the needs of the family of Nazareth
and girt it about with his protection, he should now
cover with the cloak of his heavenly patronage and
defend the Church of Jesus Christ.

– POPE LEO XIII

St. Oliver Plunkett, pray for us!

July 12

In paradise, St. Joseph's purity
increases the luster of Mary's.

– ST. MARY MAGDALEN DE PAZZI

Sts. Louis and Zélie Martin, pray for us!

July 13

What prudence was required always to act as the presumptive father of Jesus, not really being his father! What prudence was required to be a guide to Blessed Mary, who obeyed him in all things!

– BLESSED WILLIAM JOSEPH CHAMINADE

St. Teresa of the Andes, pray for us!

July 14

The divine house which Joseph ruled with the authority of a father, contained within its limits the scarce-born Church.

– POPE LEO XIII

St. Kateri Tekakwitha, pray for us!

July 15

He [St. Joseph] lived content in his poverty.

– ST. BONAVENTURE

St. Bonaventure, pray for us!

July 16

If you compare St. Joseph to the whole Church of Christ, is he not the special and chosen being of whom and under whom the Lord was introduced into the world with becoming dignity?

– St. Bernardine of Siena

Our Lady of Mt. Carmel, pray for us!

July 17

On the Day of Judgment, the condemned will weep bitterly for not having realized how powerful and efficacious a means of salvation they might have had in the intercession of St. Joseph.

– Venerable Mary of Agreda

St. Clelia Barbieri, pray for us!

July 18

The Eternal Father shares with St. Joseph the authority which he has over the Incarnate Word, just as God shared with Adam his authority over creatures.

– BLESSED WILLIAM JOSEPH CHAMINADE

St. Camillus de Lellis, pray for us!

July 19

Joseph, Jesus, and Mary — a trinity worthy indeed to be honored and greatly esteemed!

– ST. FRANCIS DE SALES

Blessed Juliette Verolot, pray for us!

July 20

Glorious St. Joseph, model of all who work, obtain for me the grace to work conscientiously, putting the call of duty above my many sins; to work with gratitude and joy, considering it an honor to employ and develop, by my labor, the gifts received from God.

– ST. POPE PIUS X

Blessed Marie-Geneviève Meunier, pray for us!

July 21

In any kingdom not only the king and queen, who shine forth in the kingdom like the sun and the moon, but also the kingdom's princes, dukes, governors, etc., and especially the parents and blood relatives of the king, who shine like the stars in the sky, are held in honor by the king's good and faithful subjects. So, my friends, reason certainly demands that in this kingdom of Christ not only Christ and the Blessed Virgin be worthy of high esteem, but also all the saints and especially this blessed man, Joseph, the father of Christ and spouse of the most holy Virgin, be held in highest honor by Christ himself as his father and by the most holy Virgin as her husband.

– St. Lawrence of Brindisi

St. Lawrence of Brindisi, pray for us!

July 22

To be just is, indeed, to be perfectly united to the
Divine Will, and to be always conformed to it in all
sorts of events, whether prosperous or adverse.
That St. Joseph was this, no one can doubt.

— ST. FRANCIS DE SALES

Blessed Madeline-Claudine Ledoine, pray for us!

July 23

So perfectly was he [St. Joseph] dead to the world
and the flesh, that he desired nothing
but the things of heaven.

— ST. BRIDGET OF SWEDEN

St. Bridget of Sweden, pray for us!

July 24

He [St. Joseph] will be the spiritual director of my
interior life, in order that I may lead that same
life with him, hidden with Jesus and Mary.

– St. Peter Julian Eymard

St. Charbel Makhluf, pray for us!

July 25

See how the Angel moulds him [St. Joseph] like
wax in his hands! He tells him that he must go into
Egypt; he goes. He commands him to return into
his own country; he returns.

– St. Francis de Sales

Blessed Maria Mercedes Prat, pray for us!

July 26

Fathers and mothers of families have in
St. Joseph and in St. Anne models of love
and service to the Queen of Heaven.

— BLESSED GABRIELE ALLEGRA

Sts. Joachim and Anne, pray for us!

July 27

O how I love to call St. Joseph the patriarch of
Christians and of the elect of God! And why would
we not confer on him this venerable name, he who
was always called the father of Jesus; he who was
the true husband of Mary; he especially who
played such a part in the mysteries of our
spiritual regeneration?

— BLESSED WILLIAM JOSEPH CHAMINADE

Blessed Titus Brandsma, pray for us!

July 28

Oh, how many and what tender kisses his [Jesus']
sacred lips bestowed on him [St. Joseph], to reward
him for his toil and labors!

— ST. FRANCIS DE SALES

St. Alphonsa of the Immaculate Conception, pray for us!

July 29

He [Jesus] indeed enriched him [St. Joseph]
and filled him to overflowing with entirely unique
graces, enabling him to execute most faithfully
the duties of so sublime a state.

— BLESSED POPE PIUS IX

Blessed Paul Tcheng, pray for us!

July 30

Would that I could make known all the signal graces which God has showered upon me, and all the dangers of soul and body from which I have been delivered, through the intercession of this great saint.

– St. Teresa of Avila

Blessed Maria Vicenta Chavez Orozco, pray for us!

July 31

Let all persons … learn from Joseph to consider present passing affairs in the light of future good which will endure forever, and find consolation amid human vicissitudes in the hope of heavenly things, so that they may aspire to them in a manner conformable to the divine will — that is, by living soberly, justly, and piously.

– Pope Benedict XV

St. Ignatius of Loyola, pray for us!

AUGUST

August 1

Saint Joseph is most powerful against the demons
which fight against us at the end of our lives.

– St. Alphonsus Liguori

St. Alphonsus Liguori, pray for us!

August 2

In vain do we look for a saint who has been honored
with a dignity the equal of St. Joseph's.

– St. Peter Julian Eymard

St. Peter Julian Eymard, pray for us!

August 3

May St. Joseph become for all of us an exceptional teacher in the service of Christ's saving mission.

– ST. JOHN PAUL II

Blessed Frédéric Janssoone, pray for us!

August 4

My dear St. Joseph, be with me living, be with me dying, and obtain for me a favorable judgment from Jesus, my merciful Savior.

– POPE LEO XIII

St. John Vianney, pray for us!

August 5

Because of the sublime dignity which God
conferred on his most faithful servant [St. Joseph],
the Church has always most highly honored and
praised Blessed Joseph next to his spouse, the
Virgin Mother of God, and has besought his
intercession in times of trouble.

– BLESSED POPE PIUS IX

Blessed Miroslav Bulešić, pray for us!

August 6

As regards his [St. Joseph's] constancy, did he not display
it wonderfully when, seeing Our Lady with child, and
not knowing how that could be, his mind was tossed
with distress, perplexity, and trouble? Yet, in spite of all,
he never complained, he was never harsh or ungracious
towards his holy spouse, but remained just as gentle and
respectful in his demeanor as he had ever been.

– ST. FRANCIS DE SALES

Blessed Engelmar Unzeitig, pray for us!

August 7

As that former Joseph was the beloved of his father
[see Gen 37:3], so this Joseph is the beloved of God.

– St. Lawrence of Brindisi

Blessed Edmund Bojanowski, pray for us!

August 8

Get to know Joseph and you will find Jesus.
Talk to Joseph and you will find Mary.

– St. Josemaria Escriva

St. Dominic, pray for us!

August 9

God chose to make Joseph his most tangible image on earth, the depository of all the rights of his divine paternity, the husband of that noble Virgin who is Mistress of angels and men.

– BLESSED WILLIAM JOSEPH CHAMINADE

St. Teresa Benedicta of the Cross, pray for us!

August 10

He [St. Joseph] won for himself the title of "The Just Man," and thus serves as a living model of that Christian justice which should reign in social life.

– POPE PIUS XI

Blessed Claudio Granzotto, pray for us!

August 11

Saint Joseph was "a just man," a tireless worker, the
upright guardian of those entrusted to his care.

– St. John Paul II

Blessed Karl Leisner, pray for us!

August 12

Valiant and strong is the man who, like St.
Joseph, perseveres in humility; he will be
conqueror at once of the devil and of the world,
which is full of ambition, vanity and pride.

– St. Francis de Sales

St. Jane Frances de Chantal, pray for us!

August 13

It is true that the other saints enjoy great power in heaven, but they ask as servants, and do not command as masters. Saint Joseph, to whose authority Jesus was subject on earth, obtains what he desires from his kingly foster Son in heaven.

– St. Thomas Aquinas

Blessed Isidore Bakanja, pray for us!

August 14

With the exception of our loving Mother, St. Joseph stands above all the saints.

– St. Maximilian Kolbe

St. Maximilian Kolbe, pray for us!

August 15

Saint Joseph is in heaven, body and soul,
there is no doubt about that.

– St. Francis de Sales

Mary, Assumed into Heaven, pray for us!

August 16

What a sublime vision to have the Son of God
ever before his [St. Joseph's] eyes! Ecstasy most
rare! Rapture most marvelous!

– Blessed William Joseph Chaminade

Blessed Antoine-Frédéric Ozanam, pray for us!

August 17

Jesus granted to him [St. Joseph] the special privilege of safeguarding the dying against the snares of Lucifer, just as he had also saved him from the schemes of Herod.

– ST. ALPHONSUS LIGUORI

St. Jeanne Delanoue, pray for us!

August 18

You would think that to protect this precious treasure [Jesus], the omnipotent God would equip him [St. Joseph] with thunderbolts. Wrong. Joseph sees in his arms a fugitive God and he follows him. He finds consolation only in his submission and in his confidence.

– BLESSED WILLIAM JOSEPH CHAMINADE

St. Alberto Hurtado, pray for us!

August 19

Joseph can tell us many things about Jesus.
Therefore, never neglect devotion to him.

– St. Josemaria Escriva

St. John Eudes, pray for us!

August 20

Who and what manner of man this blessed Joseph was,
you may conjecture from the name by which, a dispensa-
tion being allowed, he deserved to be so honored as to be
believed and to be called the father of God. You may conjecture it from his very name, which, being interpreted, means
"Increase." At the same time, remember that great man, the
former patriarch, who was sold into Egypt; and know that
Joseph not only inherited the latter's name, but attained to
his chastity, and equaled his grace and innocence.

– St. Bernard of Clairvaux

St. Bernard of Clairvaux, pray for us!

August 21

O Joseph, virgin father of Jesus, most pure spouse of the
Virgin Mary, pray for us daily to the same Jesus, the Son
of God, that armed with the weapons of his grace, we
may fight as we ought during life, and be crowned by
him at the moment of our death.

– St. Pope Pius X

St. Pope Pius X, pray for us!

August 22

He [St. Joseph] is able to obtain from our Queen,
Mary, all that is lacking to us, all that we have need of,
even in the temporal order, and he wishes us to have
all manner of good things. Let us then have for him,
my dear children, a truly filial devotion, and may his
blessed name be in our hearts always and on our lips,
along with those of Jesus and Mary.

– Blessed William Joseph Chaminade

Queen of Heaven, pray for us!

August 23

He [St. Joseph] most diligently reared him
whom the faithful were to receive as the bread
that came down from heaven whereby they
might obtain eternal life.

— BLESSED POPE PIUS IX

St. Rose of Lima, pray for us!

August 24

There is no doubt at all that St. Joseph was endowed with all gifts and graces required by the charge which the Eternal Father willed to commit to him, over all the domestic and temporal concerns of our Lord, and the guidance of his family, which was composed of three persons only, representing to us the mystery of the Most Holy and Adorable Trinity. Not that there is any real comparison in this matter excepting as regards our Lord, who is one of the persons of the Most Blessed Trinity, for the others were but creatures; yet still we may say that it was a trinity on earth representing in some sort the Most Holy Trinity.

– St. Francis de Sales

St. Joseph Calasanz, pray for us!

August 25

If God, as I firmly believe, so sanctified all the patriarchs
because the Messiah was to be born from them, and
sanctified all the prophets to foretell mysteries concerning
the Messiah, and sanctified Jeremiah in the womb, and
filled John the Baptist with the Holy Spirit to be the
herald of the Messiah, and above all sanctified the Blessed
Virgin to be the mother of Christ, why would he
not also sanctify Joseph, the father of Christ?

– St. Lawrence of Brindisi

St. Louis IX, pray for us!

August 26

O what a saint is the glorious St. Joseph!

– St. Francis de Sales

St. Teresa of Jesús Jornet Ibars, pray for us!

August 27

O St. Joseph, guardian of Jesus, chaste spouse of
Mary, you who passed your life in the perfect fulfill-
ment of duty, sustaining the Holy Family of Nazareth
with the work of your hands, kindly keep those who
with total trust now come to you.

– ST. POPE JOHN XXIII

St. Monica, pray for us!

August 28

Just as she [Mary] was virginally the wife, so
was he [St. Joseph] virginally the husband;
and just as she was virginally the mother, so
was he virginally the father.

– ST. AUGUSTINE

St. Augustine, pray for us!

August 29

He [St. Joseph] was a virgin, and his virginity
was the faithful mirror of the virginity of Mary.

– BLESSED JOHN HENRY NEWMAN

Blessed Laurentia Herasymiv, pray for us!

August 30

Is it not an incomparable honor for
St. Joseph to be the father of a Son who
is also the only Son of God?

– BLESSED WILLIAM JOSEPH CHAMINADE

Blessed Alfredo Ildefonso Schuster, pray for us!

August 31

Those souls most sensitive to the impulses of
divine love have rightly seen in Joseph a
brilliant example of the interior life.

– ST. JOHN PAUL II

Blessed Diego Ventaja Milán, pray for us!

SEPTEMBER

September 1

Him whom countless kings and prophets desired
to see, Joseph not only saw but conversed with,
and embraced in paternal affection, and kissed.

– BLESSED POPE PIUS IX

Blessed Dominic of Nagasaki, pray for us!

September 2

Because St. Joseph was associated with Mary in her
glorious privileges, he also had to suffer like her, and
his heart, too, was pierced by seven swords.

– ST. PETER JULIAN EYMARD

Blessed Anthony Ishida, pray for us!

September 3

All for Jesus, all for Mary, all to imitate you,
O patriarch St. Joseph. This shall be
my motto for life and eternity.

– ST. POPE PIUS X

Blessed Brigida of Jesus, pray for us!

September 4

Let us pray to St. Joseph
with all fervor and confidence.

– BLESSED WILLIAM JOSEPH CHAMINADE

Blessed Dina Bélanger, pray for us!

September 5

Why was St. Matthew so keen to note Joseph's trust
in the words received from the messenger of God, if
not to invite us to imitate this same loving trust?

– POPE BENEDICT XVI

Blessed Jean-Joseph Lataste, pray for us!

September 6

Saint Joseph's dignity springs from his privilege of
being the legal father of the Incarnate Son of God.
Here, then, is a man whom the Son of God calls father,
one whom he [Jesus] serves and obeys and before
whom he kneels for a paternal blessing.

– ST. PETER JULIAN EYMARD

Blessed Odoardo Focherini, pray for us!

September 7

Joseph had of necessity to die before the Lord,
for he could not have endured his crucifixion;
he was too gentle, too loving.

— BLESSED ANNE CATHERINE EMMERICH

Blessed Eugenia Picco, pray for us!

September 8

I beseech all the faithful children of the Church to be
very devoted to him [St. Joseph].

— VENERABLE MARY OF AGREDA

Blessed Alan de la Roche, pray for us!

September 9

He [St. Joseph] had a right over all the riches of his Son, and these were the treasures of the Divinity. He had a right too over the goods of his spouse, who was richer by far than all the saints together.

– ST. PETER JULIAN EYMARD

St. Peter Claver, pray for us!

September 10

God was pleased to take to himself St. Joseph before our Savior's Passion, to spare him the overwhelming grief it would have caused him.

– ST. BERNARDINE OF SIENA

Blessed Pierre Bonhomme, pray for us!

September 11

Aid us from on high, most valiant defender, in this conflict with the powers of darkness, and even as of old thou didst rescue the child Jesus from the peril of his life, so now defend God's holy Church from the snares of the enemy and from all adversity.

– POPE LEO XIII

St. John-Gabriel Perboyre, pray for us!

September 12

The name of Joseph will be our protection during all the days of our life, but above all at the moment of death.

– BLESSED WILLIAM JOSEPH CHAMINADE

Blessed Thomas Zumarraga, pray for us!

September 13

He [St. Joseph] is a father, says St. [John]
Chrysostom, not only by reputation but also
by deputation and by delegated authority.

– BLESSED WILLIAM JOSEPH CHAMINADE

Blessed Paolo Manna, pray for us!

September 14

He [St. Joseph] is not only a patriarch,
but the leader of the patriarchs.

– ST. FRANCIS DE SALES

St. John Chrysostom, pray for us!

September 15

We may well call St. Joseph the martyr of the hidden life, for no one ever suffered as he did. But why so much sorrow in his life? Simply because the holier a person is, the more he must suffer for the love and glory of God. Suffering is the flowering of God's grace in a soul and the triumph of the soul's love for God. Therefore, St. Joseph, the greatest of saints after Mary, suffered more than all the martyrs.

– ST. PETER JULIAN EYMARD

Our Lady of Sorrows, pray for us!

September 16

The sentiments of sorrow which he [St. Joseph] felt over the loss of Christ indicated true fatherly affection in him.

– ST. BERNARDINE OF SIENA

Blessed Carlo Eraña Guruceta, pray for us!

September 17

Make him [St. Joseph] responsible for the protection
of your person, he who saved the life of his Savior.
May he take charge of the affair of your salvation.
Just as he led the Son of God in his travels, may he be
your guide on the voyage of this life until you arrive
at the haven of eternal happiness.

— BLESSED WILLIAM JOSEPH CHAMINADE

St. Robert Bellarmine, pray for us!

September 18

The Son of Joseph [Jesus] is the Master of all things,
the giver of all goods, the God of heaven and earth.

— BLESSED WILLIAM JOSEPH CHAMINADE

St. Joseph of Cupertino, pray for us!

September 19

In the Holy Family he [St. Joseph]
represented the heavenly Father.

– BLESSED JAMES ALBERIONE

St. Agatha Yi, pray for us!

September 20

I don't agree with the traditional picture of St. Joseph as
an old man, even though it may have been prompted by
a desire to emphasize the perpetual virginity of Mary. I
see him as a strong, young man, perhaps a few years older
than Our Lady, but in the prime of his life and work.

– ST. JOSEMARIA ESCRIVA

St. Paul Chong Hasang, pray for us!

September 21

Joseph is poor, and he busies himself with a
mechanical occupation whereby he earns his bread
at the sweat of his brow. He loves poverty.

– BLESSED WILLIAM JOSEPH CHAMINADE

St. François Jaccard, pray for us!

September 22

Joseph listened to the angel of the Lord and
responded to God's call to care for Jesus and Mary.
In this way he played his part in God's plan, and
became a blessing not only for the Holy Family,
but a blessing for all of humanity.

– POPE FRANCIS

St. Thomas of Villanova, pray for us!

September 23

Saint Joseph, teach me how to pray.

– ST. BERNADETTE SOUBIROUS

St. Padre Pio, pray for us!

September 24

He [a servant of St. Joseph] will beg of him the grace of dying as he himself did, with the kiss of Jesus and in the arms of Mary.

– BLESSED WILLIAM JOSEPH CHAMINADE

Blessed Anton Martin Slomšek, pray for us!

September 25

Let us praise and thank Christ for having drawn so close to us, and for giving us Joseph as an example and model of love for him.

– Pope Benedict XVI

Blessed Louis Tezza, pray for us!

September 26

Whereas Adam and Eve were the source of evil which was unleashed on the world, Joseph and Mary are the summit from which holiness spreads over the earth. The Savior began the work of salvation by this virginal and holy union.

– BLESSED POPE PAUL VI

Blessed Pope Paul VI, pray for us!

September 27

In a life of faithful performance of everyday duties, he left an example for all those who must gain their bread by the toil of their hands.

– POPE PIUS XI

St. Vincent de Paul, pray for us!

September 28

Jesus and Mary not only bent their wills to Joseph's,
for he was head of the Holy Family, but they lovingly
surrendered their hearts to him as well.

— St. Peter Julian Eymard

St. Simón de Rojas, pray for us!

September 29

The angel of the Lord revealed to Joseph the dangers
which threatened Jesus and Mary, forcing them to flee to
Egypt and then to settle in Nazareth. So too, in our time,
God calls upon us to recognize the dangers threatening
our own families and to protect them from harm.

— Pope Francis

Sts. Michael, Gabriel, and Raphael, pray for us!

September 30

Certain people who follow the ravings of the apocrypha fancy that the brethren of the Lord are sons of Joseph from another wife, and invent a certain woman, Melcha or Escha. As it is contained in the book which we wrote against Helvidius, we understand as brethren of the Lord not the sons of Joseph but the cousins of the Savior, children of Mary [of Clopas, she who was] the Lord's maternal aunt, who is said to be the mother of James the Less and Joseph and Jude. They, as we read, were called brethren of the Lord in another passage of the gospel. Indeed, all scripture indicates that cousins are called brethren.

– St. Jerome

St. Jerome, pray for us!

OCTOBER

October 1

When God wishes to raise a soul to greater heights, he unites it to St. Joseph by giving it a strong love for the good saint.

– St. Peter Julian Eymard

St. Thérèse of Lisieux, pray for us!

October 2

Be always our protector [St. Joseph]. May your interior spirit of peace, of silence, of good works, and of prayer, in the service of the Church, animate us always and make us rejoice, in union with your blessed spouse, our most sweet and Immaculate Mother, in a most strong and sweet love of Jesus, the glorious and immortal king of ages and peoples.

– St. Pope John XXIII

Holy Guardian Angels, pray for us!

October 3

Like Joseph, do not be afraid to
take Mary into your home.

– POPE BENEDICT XVI

Blessed Columba Marmion, pray for us!

October 4

O Joseph, virgin father of Jesus, most pure spouse of the
Virgin Mary, pray for us daily to the Son of God, that, armed
with the weapons of his grace, we may fight as we
ought in life, and be crowned by him in death.

– ST. BERNARDINE OF SIENA

St. Francis of Assisi, pray for us!

October 5

Saint Joseph urged me to have a constant devotion to him. He himself told me to recite three prayers [the Our Father, Hail Mary, and Glory be] and the *Memorare* [to St. Joseph] once every day. He looked at me with great kindness and gave me to know how much he is supporting this work [of Divine Mercy]. He has promised me this special help and protection. I recite the requested prayers every day and feel his special protection.

– ST. FAUSTINA KOWALSKA

St. Faustina Kowalska, pray for us!

October 6

Grant that we may not lose sight of Jesus, who busied himself with you at your carpenter's bench.

– VENERABLE POPE PIUS XII

Blessed Bartolo Longo, pray for us!

October 7

May he [St. Joseph] obtain for us the ability of
St. Dominic, St. Vincent Ferrer, and Blessed Alan
de la Roche to promote the rosary.

— BLESSED GABRIELE ALLEGRA

Our Lady of the Rosary, pray for us!

October 8

We believe that just as the mother of Jesus was a virgin,
so was Joseph, because he [God] placed the Virgin in
the care of a virgin, and just as he did this at the close
[at the Cross], so did he do it at the beginning.

— ST. THOMAS AQUINAS

Blessed Marie-Rose Durocher, pray for us!

October 9

He [St. Joseph] was the true and worthy spouse
of Mary, supplying in a visible manner the place
of Mary's invisible spouse, the Holy Spirit.

— BLESSED JOHN HENRY NEWMAN

Blessed John Henry Newman, pray for us!

October 10

Why should the "fatherly" love of Joseph not have had an influence upon the "filial" love of Jesus? And vice versa, why should the "filial" love of Jesus not have had an influence upon the "fatherly" love of Joseph, thus leading to a further deepening of their unique relationship?

— ST. JOHN PAUL II

Blessed Diego Luis de San Vitores, pray for us!

October 11

[Saint] Pope John XXIII, who had a great devotion to St. Joseph, directed that Joseph's name be inserted in the Roman Canon of Mass — which is the perpetual memorial of redemption — after the name of Mary and before the apostles, popes and martyrs.

— ST. JOHN PAUL II

St. Pope John XXIII, pray for us!

October 12

Let us picture him [St. Joseph] and imagine how
Our Lady, touched by our prayer, will get us
the grace to know and to imitate St. Joseph,
her dear and holy husband, who so much
resembled her in the practice of every virtue!

— BLESSED GABRIELE ALLEGRA

St. Daniel Comboni, pray for us!

October 13

After Our Lady had disappeared into the immense
distance of the firmament, we beheld St. Joseph with the
Child Jesus and Our Lady robed in white with a blue
mantle, beside the sun. Saint Joseph and the Child Jesus
appeared to bless the world, for they traced the
Sign of the Cross with their hands.

— SERVANT OF GOD LUCIA DOS SANTOS

St. Maria Elizabeth Hesselblad, pray for us!

October 14

Saint Joseph, of the family of the kings of Judah, leads a poor and hidden life. Because he was destined to become, as it were, the governor and father of a weak and humble God, it was fitting that he should resemble him.

– BLESSED WILLIAM JOSEPH CHAMINADE

Blessed Alexandrina Maria da Costa, pray for us!

October 15

I do not remember that I ever asked him [St. Joseph] at any time for anything which he did not obtain for me. It fills me with amazement when I consider the numberless graces which God has granted me through the intercession of this blessed saint and the perils, both of body and soul, from which he has delivered me.

– ST. TERESA OF AVILA

St. Teresa of Avila, pray for us!

October 16

Consider that the Holy Spirit chose only Joseph to
be the protector of the Blessed Virgin, to be her true
husband and consequently, no created being can
equal the glory of this great saint.

— BLESSED WILLIAM JOSEPH CHAMINADE

St. Gerard Majella, pray for us!

October 17

Saint Joseph was the spouse of Mary. In the same
way, each father sees himself entrusted with the
mystery of womanhood through his wife.

— POPE BENEDICT XVI

St. Margaret Mary Alacoque, pray for us!

October 18

If God had charged you with the honorable task of choosing from among the kings a husband for the Blessed Virgin, would you not have given her the greatest mind in the world? And if he had ordered you to pick one of the saints, would you not have given her the greatest saint who ever trod the earth? Now, do you think that the Holy Spirit, who is the author of this divine marriage, is less concerned than you are to provide her with a husband suited to her merits?

– Blessed William Joseph Chaminade

St. Luke the Evangelist, pray for us!

October 19

If discouragement overwhelms you, think of the faith of Joseph; if anxiety has its grip on you, think of the hope of Joseph, that descendent of Abraham who hoped against hope; if exasperation or hatred seizes you, think of the love of Joseph, who was the first man to set eyes on the human face of God in the person of the Infant conceived by the Holy Spirit in the womb of the Virgin Mary.

– Pope Benedict XVI

St. Charles Garnier, pray for us!

October 20

To him [St. Joseph] great power has
been given in heaven and on earth.

– BLESSED WILLIAM JOSEPH CHAMINADE

St. Paul of the Cross, pray for us!

October 21

We must beg for good adorers;
the Blessed Sacrament needs them to replace
St. Joseph and to imitate his life of adoration.

– ST. PETER JULIAN EYMARD

Blessed Giuseppe Puglisi, pray for us!

October 22

Besides trusting in Joseph's sure protection, the Church also trusts in his noble example, which transcends all individual states of life and serves as a model for the entire Christian community, whatever the condition and duties of each of its members may be.

– St. John Paul II

St. John Paul II, pray for us!

October 23

I thank you, O holy patriarch Joseph, because we who are incapable of even knowing how to love Jesus and our Immaculate Mother, know and rejoice that you at least loved her as she deserved to be loved, the worthy and true Mother of Jesus.

– Blessed Gabriele Allegra

Blessed Timothy Giaccardo, pray for us!

October 24

O glorious St. Joseph, pray for me, assist me and
defend me from Satan at the hour of my death.

– St. Anthony Mary Claret

St. Anthony Mary Claret, pray for us!

October 25

I have taken for my advocate and protector, the glorious
St. Joseph, to whom I have recommended myself with all
the fervor of my heart, and by whom I have been visibly
aided. This tender father of my soul, this loving protector
hastened to snatch me from the wretched state in which
my body languished, as he had delivered me from greater
dangers of another nature, which threatened
my honor and my eternal salvation.

– St. Teresa of Avila

Blessed Maria Restituta Kafka, pray for us!

October 26

Because of this holy and virginal marriage
with Christ's mother, Joseph merited to be
called the very father of Christ.

– St. Augustine

Blessed Anna Maria Adorni, pray for us!

October 27

I often explain that if a dove drops a date from its beak
into a garden, we say that the palm tree that grows from
that date belongs to the owner of the garden. If that is so,
who would doubt that as the Holy Spirit, like a heavenly
dove, let fall a divine seed into the "garden enclosed" of
the Blessed Virgin (a sealed garden set about with the
vow of virginity and unstained chastity) and a garden that
pertained to Joseph as a wife pertains to her husband; who,
I ask, would deny that the divine Palm Tree, which bears
the fruits of immortality, belongs to the Blessed Joseph?

– St. Francis de Sales

St. Gaetano Errico, pray for us!

October 28

Will he, the great saint whom Jesus and Mary obeyed, who provided Jesus and Mary with their daily bread, be invoked in vain? No!

– ST. LUIGI GUANELLA

St. Luigi Guanella, pray for us!

October 29

In order to augment and support Mary's virginity the Eternal Father gave her a virginal companion, the great St. Joseph.

– ST. FRANCIS DE SALES

Blessed Chiara Luce Badano, pray for us!

October 30

Never forget that St. Joseph is always
standing by to protect you.

– Venerable Pope Pius XII

Blessed Jean-Michel Langevin, pray for us!

October 31

The Koran passes over Joseph in the life of Mary, but
the Moslem tradition knows his name and has some
familiarity with him. In this tradition, Joseph is made to
speak to Mary, who is a virgin. As he inquired how she
conceived Jesus without a father, Mary answered: "Do
you not know that God, when he created the wheat, had
no need of seed, and that God by his power made the
trees grow without the help of rain? All that God had to
do was to say, 'So be it,' and it was done."

– Venerable Fulton J. Sheen

St. Valentin Berrio-Ochoa, pray for us!

NOVEMBER

November 1

Some saints, says the Angelic Doctor [St. Thomas Aquinas], have received from God the power to help us in some specific need. But the influence of St. Joseph knows no limit. His power is universal and extends to all sorts of needs and to all kinds of circumstances.

– BLESSED WILLIAM JOSEPH CHAMINADE

All Saints, pray for us!

November 2

It may be piously believed that at the moment of his [St. Joseph's] death, Jesus and the most Blessed Virgin, his spouse, were present. What exhortations! What consoling words! What promises! What luminous and enflamed words! In this moment of his passage toward eternity, what revelations on eternal goods must he have received from his most holy spouse and from Jesus, the most loving Son of God! I leave the contemplation and consideration of all this to your own devotion.

– ST. BERNARDINE OF SIENA

St. Joseph, patron of a happy death, pray for us!

November 3

Day after day, at home and in the carpenter shop, his [St. Joseph's] eyes rested on Jesus; he protected him against the dangers of childhood; he guided his advancing years; and by hard work and with religious devotedness, he provided for the increasing needs of the Mother and the Son.

– VENERABLE POPE PIUS XII

Blessed Aimée-Adèle le Bouteiller, pray for us!

November 4

This glorious saint [Joseph] has great influence in heaven with him who raised him there in body and in soul.

– ST. FRANCIS DE SALES

St. Charles Borromeo, pray for us!

November 5

Saint Joseph is the patron and protector of a happy death. Those who pray to him are certain to die in good dispositions. He is the model of those who wish to die in the Lord.

– St. Peter Julian Eymard

St. Guido Maria Conforti, pray for us!

November 6

O my beloved St. Joseph, adopt me as thy child, pray for my salvation, watch over me day and night, that I may be preserved from occasions of sin; obtain for me purity of body and soul, and the gift of prayer, through thy intercession with Jesus!

– Pope Leo XIII

Blessed Anthony Baldinucci, pray for us!

November 7

In Joseph, the apparent tension between the
active and the contemplative life finds an ideal
harmony that is only possible for those who
possess the perfection of charity.

– ST. JOHN PAUL II

St. Elizabeth of the Trinity, pray for us!

November 8

He [St. Joseph] was head of the divine household
on earth with, as it were, fatherly authority; he has
the Church dedicated to his loyalty and protection.
Such a person possesses so surpassing a dignity that
no honor exists which should not be paid him.

– POPE LEO XIII

Blessed Maria Crucified Satellico, pray for us!

November 9

Joseph was a true son of a race of kings, noble
in descent, more noble in mind.

– St. Bernard of Clairvaux

Blessed Eugene Bossilkov, pray for us!

November 10

It is a monstrous crime for a father to be poor while the
son lives in abundance. Who could imagine that the Son
of God, who is master of all virtues, would forget Joseph
whom he loved and cherished as his father? He [Jesus]
must have spared no effort to enrich him [with virtues].

– Blessed William Joseph Chaminade

St. Gregory Palamas, pray for us!

November 11

The Church encourages us to prepare ourselves for the hour of our death. In the ancient litany of the saints, for instance, she has us pray: "From a sudden and unforeseen death, deliver us, O Lord," to ask the Mother of God to intercede for us "at the hour of our death" in the *Hail Mary*, and to entrust ourselves to St. Joseph, the patron of a happy death.

– Catechism of the Catholic Church

Blessed Kamen Vitchev, pray for us!

November 12

I have prayed to our Lord that he might give me St. Joseph for a father, as he had given me Mary for a mother; that he might put in my heart that devotion, that confidence, that filial love of a client, of a devotee of St. Joseph. I trust the good Master has heard my prayers, for I now feel greater devotion to this great saint, and I am full of confidence and hope.

– St. Peter Julian Eymard

Blessed Gregory Lakota, pray for us!

November 13

To you, O Blessed Joseph, we come in our trials, and having asked the help of your most holy spouse, we confidently ask your patronage, also.

– POPE LEO XIII

St. Stanislaus Kostka, pray for us!

November 14

Joseph shines among all mankind by the most august dignity, since by divine will, he was the guardian of the Son of God and reputed as his father among men.

– POPE LEO XIII

St. Frances Xavier Cabrini, pray for us!

November 15

As a virginal husband, he [St. Joseph] guarded his virginal wife.

– ST. ALBERT THE GREAT

St. Albert the Great, pray for us!

November 16

I saw heaven opened and St. Joseph sitting upon a magnificent throne. I felt myself wonderfully affected when, each time his name was mentioned, all the saints made a profound inclination toward him, showing by the serenity and sweetness of their looks that they rejoiced with him on account of his exalted dignity.

– St. Gertrude the Great

St. Gertrude the Great, pray for us!

November 17

Remember, most pure spouse of the Blessed Virgin Mary, my loving protector, St. Joseph, that no one ever had recourse to thy protection, implored thy help, or sought thy mediation without obtaining relief. Confiding, therefore, in thy goodness, I come before thee and fervently recommend myself to thy care and protection. Oh despise not, most loving foster father of my Redeemer, the petition of thy humble client, but graciously hear and grant it. Amen.

– Blessed Pope Pius IX

St. Giuseppe Moscati, pray for us!

November 18

He [St. Joseph] is truly the saint
who carried out his duty in silence
but with angelic fervor.

– BLESSED GABRIELE ALLEGRA

St. Rose Philippine Duchesne, pray for us!

November 19

Those who are devoted to prayer should, in a special
manner, cherish devotion to St. Joseph. I know not
how anyone can ponder on the sufferings, trials and
tribulations the Queen of Angels endured whilst
caring for Jesus in his childhood, without at the same
time thanking St. Joseph for the services he rendered
the Divine Child and his Blessed Mother.

– ST. TERESA OF AVILA

Blessed Karolina Kózka, pray for us!

November 20

Now if holiness consists in grace and grace consists in charity, and charity consists in faith in Christ and love for Christ, who of all the saints after the Blessed Virgin had a greater love for Christ than Joseph?

— St. Lawrence of Brindisi

Blessed Salvatore Lilli, pray for us!

November 21

O most intimate familiarity to be always with God, to speak only to God, to work, to rest, to converse in the company and presence of God! How many times did the happy tutor of the Child Jesus, like a chaste bee, gather the nectar of pure devotion from this beautiful flower of Jesse? How many times did he [St. Joseph], like the dove, hide in the heart of this rock?

— Blessed William Joseph Chaminade

Blessed Franciszka Siedliska, pray for us!

November 22

He [St. Joseph] never preached, but he gave his entire life to the service of Jesus and died in his arms. If Jesus cried over Lazarus, must he not have cried over [the death of] St. Joseph?

– St. Peter Julian Eymard

Blessed Toros Oghlou David, pray for us!

November 23

O faithful guardian of the Mother of God, keep those who honor you amid the trials and joys of this life. Lovable tutor of Jesus, help your servants in the dangers and difficulties of their exile; may they feel the effects of your love. Obtain for them devotion to your spouse, fidelity to your Son, unfailing respect for the Eternal Father who reigns with the Holy Spirit through endless ages.

– Blessed William Joseph Chaminade

Blessed Miguel Agustin Pro, pray for us!

November 24

No other distinction can surpass that of having received [as St. Joseph did] the revelation of the hypostatic union of the divine Word.

– POPE PIUS XI

Blessed Maria Anna Sala, pray for us!

November 25

A servant of Mary will have a tender devotion to St. Joseph, and by his pious homage of respect and love, will endeavor to merit the protection of this great saint.

– BLESSED WILLIAM JOSEPH CHAMINADE

Blesseds Luigi and Maria Beltrame Quattrocchi, pray for us!

November 26

Joseph worked assiduously as the natural and
divine law requires, with a supernatural spirit,
performing humble work, content with his state
in life and with his modest income.

– BLESSED JAMES ALBERIONE

Blessed James Alberione, pray for us!

November 27

Rejoice, devout servants of St. Joseph, for you are close
to paradise; the ladder leading up to it has but three
rungs, Jesus, Mary, Joseph. Here is how one climbs up or
down this ladder. As you climb up, your requests are first
placed in the hands of St. Joseph, St. Joseph hands them
over to Mary, and Mary to Jesus. As you climb down, the
responses came from Jesus, Jesus delivers them to Mary,
and Mary hands them over to Joseph.

– ST. LEONARD OF PORT MAURICE

St. Leonard of Port Maurice, pray for us!

November 28

Picture to yourself the sanctity of all the patriarchs of old, that long line of successive generations which is the mysterious ladder of Jacob, culminating in the person of the Son of God. See how great was the faith of Abraham, the obedience of Isaac, the courage of David, the wisdom of Solomon. After you have formed the highest opinion of these saints, remember that Joseph is at the top of the ladder, at the head of the saints, the kings, the prophets, the patriarchs, that he is more faithful than Abraham, more obedient than Isaac, more generous that David, wiser than Solomon, in a word, as superior in grace as he is close to the source, Jesus sleeping in his arms.

– BLESSED WILLIAM JOSEPH CHAMINADE

St. Catherine Labouré, pray for us!

November 29

He [St. Joseph] was always imperturbable, even in
adversities. Let us model ourselves after this sublime
example and let us learn to remain peaceful
and tranquil in all of life's circumstances.

– ST. JOSEPH MARELLO

St. John Berchmans, pray for us!

November 30

The Gospel does not record a single word from
him; his language is silence.

– BLESSED POPE PAUL VI

St. Joseph Marchand, pray for us!

DECEMBER

December 1

The confidence should be very great which we ought to bear toward this saint [St. Joseph], founded as it is on such prolonged and even unique relationships with the very sources of grace and of life, the Blessed Trinity.

– POPE PIUS XI

Blessed Charles de Foucauld, pray for us!

December 2

The Church also calls upon Joseph as her protector because of a profound and ever present desire to reinvigorate her ancient life with true evangelical virtues, such as shine forth in St. Joseph.

– BLESSED POPE PAUL VI

St. Edmund Campion, pray for us!

December 3

If Christ sits at the right hand of his Father in the glory of
paradise above all the choirs of angels, because he is the
first of all the predestined and was the holiest of the holiest
in this world, and if the Blessed Virgin, by reason of her
own holiness, holds the second place after Christ because
she is also second by reason of predestination from eternity
and grace in time, it seems to me that because Joseph holds
the third place after Christ in eternal predestination and
grace in time, so by the same reasoning he also holds the
third place in the glory of paradise.

– St. Lawrence of Brindisi

Blessed Marie-Clémentine Anuarite Nengapeta, pray for us!

December 4

Jesus slept with the protection of Joseph.

– Pope Francis

St. Giovanni Calabria, pray for us!

December 5

Devotion to St. Joseph is one of the choicest graces
that God can give to a soul, for it is tantamount to
revealing the entire treasury of our Lord's graces.

– St. Peter Julian Eymard

Blessed Philip Rinaldi, pray for us!

December 6

To fathers of families, Joseph is a superlative
model of paternal vigilance and care.

– Pope Leo XIII

Blessed Adolph Kolping, pray for us!

December 7

How numerous and how exalted were the virtues
with which he [God] adorned his [St. Joseph's] poor
and humble condition! And among all these virtues
none was wanting to ennoble the man who was to be
the husband of Mary Immaculate and who was to be
thought the father of our Lord Jesus Christ.

– POPE BENEDICT XV

Blessed John Duns Scotus, pray for us!

December 8

He [St. Joseph] witnesses to Mary's Immaculate life
and her amiability even before her son was born.

– VENERABLE FULTON J. SHEEN

Immaculate Mary, pray for us!

December 9

Through that sacred bond of charity which united
you [St. Joseph] to the Immaculate Virgin Mother
of God and through the fatherly love with which you
embraced the Child Jesus, we humbly beg you to
look graciously upon the beloved inheritance which
Jesus Christ purchased by his blood, and to aid us in
our necessities with your power and strength.

– POPE LEO XIII

St. Juan Diego, pray for us!

December 10

How hard he [St. Joseph] must have prayed to
come to know and ever increase in love toward
his immaculate wife.

– BLESSED GABRIELE ALLEGRA

Blessed Marcantonio Durando, pray for us!

December 11

The Church's constant tradition holds that St. Joseph lived a life of consecrated chastity. Some of the apocryphal gospels picture him as an old man, even a widower. This is not the Church's teaching. We are rather to believe that he was a virgin, who entered into a virginal marriage with Mary.

– SERVANT OF GOD JOHN A. HARDON

Blessed László Batthyány-Strattmann, pray for us!

December 12

Let us imitate our heavenly Patroness [Mary] in our attitude toward St. Joseph. Though her own dignity was so exalted, she honored his virtues, and she fulfilled this duty, even as she received great revelations from on high and saw their accomplishment day after day.

– BLESSED WILLIAM JOSEPH CHAMINADE

Our Lady of Guadalupe, pray for us!

December 13

Saint Joseph, more than anyone else before or since, learned from Jesus to be alert to recognize God's wonders, to have his mind and heart awake. But if Joseph learned from Jesus to live in a divine way, I would be bold enough to say that humanly speaking, there was much he taught God's Son. There is something I do not quite like in that title of foster father which is sometimes given to Joseph, because it might make us think of the relationship between Joseph and Jesus as something cold and external. Certainly our faith tells us that he was not his father according to the flesh, but this is not the only kind of fatherhood.

– St. Josemaria Escriva

Blessed José María of Manila, pray for us!

December 14

Saint Joseph, pray that my love for the Child Jesus may increase. Be a father to me!

– St. John Neumann

St. Nimatullah Kassab Al-Hardini, pray for us!

December 15

Shield us ever under thy patronage [St. Joseph], that
imitating thy example and strengthened by thy help,
we may live a holy life, die a happy death,
and attain everlasting bliss in heaven.

– POPE LEO XIII

St. Virginia Bracelli, pray for us!

December 16

God alone could grant Joseph the strength to trust
the angel. God alone will give you, dear married
couples, the strength to raise your family as he wants.

– POPE BENEDICT XVI

Blessed Clemente Marchisio, pray for us!

December 17

There were indeed heretics who thought Joseph, the husband of the ever Virgin Mary, had generated from another wife those whom Scripture calls the "brethren of the Lord." Others, with still more cunning, thought that he [St. Joseph] would have given birth to others from Mary herself after the birth of the Lord. But, my dearest brethren, without any fear on this question, we must know and confess that not only the Blessed Mother of God, but also the most holy witness and guardian of her chastity, remained free from absolutely all marital acts; in scriptural usage, the "brothers and sisters of the Lord" are called, not their children [of Mary and Joseph], but their relatives.

– ST. BEDE THE VENERABLE

St. José Manyanet y Vives, pray for us!

December 18

O you [St. Joseph] whose power reaches all our necessities, open your fatherly eyes to the needs of your children. In the confusion and pain which press upon us, we have recourse to you with confidence.

– St. Francis de Sales

Blessed María Inés Teresa
del Santísimo Sacramento, pray for us!

December 19

The cloud [that] in the Old Law overshadowed the tabernacle is a figure of St. Joseph's marriage with the Blessed Virgin. *The cloud covered the tabernacle of the covenant, and the glory of the Lord filled it* (Ex 40:32). Saint Joseph's marriage is a sacred veil which covers the mystery of the Incarnation. Everyone sees that Mary is a mother, but only Joseph knows that she is a virgin.

– Blessed William Joseph Chaminade

Blessed Maria Fortunata Viti, pray for us!

December 20

If we place our trust in him [St. Joseph], he will obtain
for us a holy increase in every virtue, especially in those
which he himself possessed in the highest degree, such
as holy purity of body and spirit, humility, constancy,
perseverance: virtues which will make us victorious over
our enemies in this life, and worthy to enjoy in the life
to come the reward prepared for those who follow the
example given them by St. Joseph.

– ST. FRANCIS DE SALES

Blessed Vladimir Ghika, pray for us!

December 21

In heaven the sovereign of angels and men still calls St.
Joseph father, while Mary, the Queen of Heaven and
earth, calls him her spouse and honors him as such.

– ST. PETER JULIAN EYMARD

Blessed Peter Friedhofen, pray for us!

December 22

Who was holier than Joseph? Who was purer than the Most Holy Virgin? And yet he [St. Joseph] wanted to leave her secretly. But how prudently and righteously he wanted to do it! He did not want to separate from her openly, lest she be defamed, but clandestinely, that she may preserve her good name. You ought to learn from this holy and just man: although the deeds of others may seem evil to you and are said to be imperfect, you should judge them secretly, not openly, and judge in such a way that neither your conscience nor their good name be hurt. If you do so, you will not be lacking the light, so that you may judge rightly, as the righteous husband of the Most Holy Virgin did not lack light for comprehending the truth about how she had conceived.

– St. Stanislaus Papczynski

Blessed María Crescencia Pérez, pray for us!

December 23

The Gospel is the revelation in Jesus Christ of God's mercy to sinners. The angel announced to Joseph: "You shall call his name Jesus, for he will save his people from their sins."

– CATECHISM OF THE CATHOLIC CHURCH

Blessed Marie-Eugène of the Child Jesus, pray for us!

December 24

He [St. Joseph] was the Cherub, placed to guard the new terrestrial paradise from the intrusion of every foe.

– BLESSED JOHN HENRY NEWMAN

St. Toribio Romo González, pray for us!

December 25

He [St. Joseph] took his [Jesus'] little hands and
raising them to heaven he said: "Stars of heaven,
behold the hands which created you; O Sun, behold
the arm that drew you out of nothingness."

– BLESSED WILLIAM JOSEPH CHAMINADE

Blessed Michael Nakashima, pray for us!

December 26

If earthly princes consider it a matter of so much
importance to select carefully a tutor fit for their
children, think you that the Eternal God would not,
in his almighty power and wisdom, choose from out of
his creation the most perfect man living [St. Joseph] to
be the guardian of his divine and most glorious Son,
the Prince of heaven and earth?

– ST. FRANCIS DE SALES

Blessed Albertina Berkenbrock, pray for us!

December 27

God called Joseph to "take Mary as your wife, for that which is conceived in her is of the Holy Spirit," so that Jesus, "who is called Christ," should be born of Joseph's spouse into the messianic lineage of David.

– CATECHISM OF THE CATHOLIC CHURCH

St. John the Apostle, pray for us!

December 28

With the increase of devotion to St. Joseph among the faithful there will necessarily result an increase in their devotion toward the Holy Family of Nazareth, of which he was the august head.

– POPE BENEDICT XV

Blessed Laura Vicuña, pray for us!

December 29

Like Jesus, we should honor St. Joseph as our
father. Our Lord gave him that beautiful title and
confirmed himself to the relation it created; he
honored, served, and loved Joseph in his capacity
as father. We should do likewise.

– ST. PETER JULIAN EYMARD

St. Thomas Becket, pray for us!

December 30

By St. Joseph we are led directly to Mary, and by
Mary to the fountain of all holiness, Jesus Christ,
who sanctified the domestic virtues of his
obedience toward St. Joseph and Mary.

– POPE BENEDICT XV

St. John Alcober, pray for us!

December 31

May St. Joseph obtain for the Church and
for the world, as well as for each of us, the blessing
of the Father, Son, and Holy Spirit.

– St. John Paul II

Blessed Álvaro del Portillo, pray for us!

LITANY OF ST. JOSEPH

Lord, have mercy. *Lord, have mercy.*
Christ, have mercy. *Christ have mercy.*
Lord, have mercy. *Lord, have mercy.*
Jesus, hear us. *Jesus, graciously hear us.*
God, the Father of Heaven, *have mercy on us.*
God the Son, Redeemer of the world, *have mercy on us.*
God the Holy Spirit, *have mercy on us.*
Holy Trinity, One God, *have mercy on us.*

Holy Mary, *pray for us.*
Saint Joseph, *pray for us.*
Noble offspring of David, *pray for us.*
Splendor of Patriarchs, *pray for us.*
Spouse of the Mother of God, *pray for us.*
Chaste guardian of the Virgin, *pray for us.*
Foster-father of the Son of God, *pray for us.*
Zealous defender of Christ, *pray for us.*
Head of the Holy Family, *pray for us.*
Joseph most just, *pray for us.*

Joseph most chaste, *pray for us.*
Joseph most prudent, *pray for us.*
Joseph most courageous, *pray for us.*
Joseph most obedient, *pray for us.*
Joseph most faithful, *pray for us.*
Mirror of patience, *pray for us.*
Lover of poverty, *pray for us.*
Model of workmen, *pray for us.*
Glory of domestic life, *pray for us.*
Guardian of virgins, *pray for us.*
Pillar of families, *pray for us.*
Comfort of the afflicted, *pray for us.*
Hope of the sick, *pray for us.*
Patron of the dying, *pray for us.*
Terror of demons, *pray for us.*
Protector of the Holy Church, *pray for us.*

Lamb of God, who takes away the sins of the world,
    Spare us, O Lord.
Lamb of God, who takes away the sins of the world,
    Graciously hear us, O Lord.
Lamb of God, who takes away the sins of the world,
    Have mercy on us.

V. He has made him master of His house,
R. And ruler of all His possessions.

Let us pray. O God, who, in your loving providence, chose Blessed Joseph to be the spouse of your most Holy Mother, grant us the favor of having him for our intercessor in heaven whom on earth we venerate as our protector. You, who live and reign forever and ever. Amen.

REFERENCES

Initial quote from Ven. Fulton J. Sheen:
Ven. Fulton J. Sheen, *The World's First Love: Mary, Mother of God.*
(San Francisco: Ignatius Press, 1996), 92.

January
Image: *Return from the Flight into Egypt (c.1640)*
Giovanni Francesco Romanelli (1610-1662)
© Colección Carmen Thyssen-Bornemisza en depósito en el Museo Thyssen-Bornemisza/Scala, Florence

January 1
St. John Paul II, *Redemptoris Custos,* 1.

January 2
St. Gregory of Nazianzen, as quoted in Antony J. Patrignani, SJ, *A Manual of Practical Devotion to St. Joseph.* (Rockford, Illinois: TAN Books, 1982), 72.

January 3
St. Bernardine of Siena, as quoted in Francis L. Filas, SJ, *Joseph and Jesus: A Theological Study of Their Relationship.* (Milwaukee: Bruce Publishing Co.), 79.

January 4
Pope Leo XIII, *Neminem Fugit,* as quoted in Francis L. Filas, SJ, *St. Joseph & Daily Christian Living.* (New York: Macmillan Co., 1959), 188.

January 5
St. John Neumann, as quoted in Joseph F. Chorpenning, OSFS, "St. Joseph's Presence in the Life and Ministry of John N. Neumann, CSsR" in *St. Joseph Studies: Papers in English from the Seventh and Eighth International St. Joseph Symposia: Malta 1997 and El Salvador 2001.* Ed. Larry Toschi, OSJ (Santa Cruz, California: Guardian of the Redeemer Books, 2002), 132.

January 6
St. André Bessette, as quoted in Henri-Paul Bergeron, CSC, *Brother Andre: The*

Wonder Man of Mount Royal. trans. Rev. Real Boudreau, CSC. (Montreal: Saint Joseph Oratory, 1997), 72.

January 7
St. Augustine, as quoted in Rev. Nicholas O'Rafferty, *Discourses on St. Joseph.* (Milwaukee: Bruce Publishing Co., 1951), 208.

January 8
St. Francis de Sales, as quoted in Rosalie Marie Levy, *Joseph the Just Man.* (Derby, New York: Daughters of St. Paul, 1955), 121.

January 9
St. Teresa of Avila, as quoted in Rev. Nicholas O'Rafferty, *Discourses on St. Joseph.* (Milwaukee: Bruce Publishing Co., 1951), 209.

January 10
St. John Paul II, *Redemptoris Custos,* 5.

January 11
St. Peter Julian Eymard, *Month of St. Joseph.* (Cleveland, Ohio: Emmanuel Publications, 1948), 5.

January 12
Blessed Pope Pius IX, *Inclytum Patriarcham* (July 7, 1871).

January 13
St. Hilary of Poitiers, as quoted in Blessed William Joseph Chaminade, *Marian Writings. Vol. 1.* ed. J.B. Armbruster, SM (Dayton, Ohio: Marianist Press, 1980), 234.

January 14
Ven. Pope Pius XII, as quoted in Francis L. Filas, SJ, *St. Joseph & Daily Christian Living.* (New York: Macmillan Co., 1959), 196.

January 15
St. Teresa of Avila, as quoted in Rosalie Marie Levy, *Joseph the Just Man.* (Derby, New York: Daughters of St. Paul, 1955), 145-146.

January 16
St. Bernardine of Siena, as quoted in Francis L. Filas, SJ, *Joseph and Jesus: A Theological Study of Their Relationship.* (Milwaukee: Bruce Publishing Co.), 79.

January 17
Blessed William Joseph Chaminade, *Marian Writings. Vol. 1.* ed. J.B. Armbruster, SM (Dayton, Ohio: Marianist Press, 1980), 229.

January 18
Catechism of the Catholic Church, par. 532.

January 19
St. Bernardine of Siena, as quoted in Antony J. Patrignani, SJ, *A Manual of Practical Devotion to St. Joseph*. (Rockford, Illinois: TAN Books, 1982), 212.

January 20
Blessed William Joseph Chaminade, *Marian Writings. Vol. 1.* ed. J.B. Armbruster, SM (Dayton, Ohio: Marianist Press, 1980), 112.

January 21
St. Albert the Great, as quoted in Francis L. Filas, SJ, *Joseph and Jesus: A Theological Study of Their Relationship*. (Milwaukee: Bruce Publishing Co.), 63.

January 22
Blessed William Joseph Chaminade, as quoted in *From a Full Heart: Thoughts from Father Chaminade* (North American Center for Marianist Studies, NACMS). Compiled by Francis J. Greiner, SM, (St. Meinard, Indiana: The Grail Press, 1949), entry for March 12.

January 23
St. John Neumann, as quoted in Joseph F. Chorpenning, OSFS, "St. Joseph's Presence in the Life and Ministry of John N. Neumann, CSsR" in *St. Joseph Studies: Papers in English from the Seventh and Eighth International St. Joseph Symposia: Malta 1997 and El Salvador 2001*. Ed. Larry Toschi, OSJ (Santa Cruz, California: Guardian of the Redeemer Books, 2002), 135.

January 24
St. Francis de Sales, as quoted in Fr. Marie-Dominique Philippe, OP, *The Mystery of Joseph*. (Bethesda, Maryland: Zaccheus Press, 2009), 153.

January 25
Pope Leo XIII, *Quamquam Pluries*, 4.

January 26
Blessed Gabriele Allegra, *Mary's Immaculate Heart: A Way to God*. (Chicago, Illinois: Franciscan Herald Press, 1983), 55.

January 27
St. Teresa of Avila, as quoted in Rosalie Marie Levy, *Joseph the Just Man*. (Derby, New York: Daughters of St. Paul, 1955), 147.

January 28
St. Thomas Aquinas, *Commentary on Matthew, I, no. 117,* as quoted in Fr.

Marie-Dominique Philippe, OP, *The Mystery of Joseph*. (Bethesda, Maryland: Zaccheus Press, 2009), 169.

January 29
St. Joseph Marello, as quoted in Larry Toschi, OSJ, *St. Joseph in the Lives of Two Blesseds of the Church: Blessed Junipero Serra and Blessed Joseph Marello*. (Santa Cruz, California: Guardian of the Redeemer Books, 1994), 75.

January 30
Blessed William Joseph Chaminade, *Marian Writings. Vol. 1*. ed. J.B. Armbruster, SM (Dayton, Ohio: Marianist Press, 1980), 227-228.

January 31
St. Thomas Aquinas, as quoted in Rev. Nicholas O'Rafferty, *Discourses on St. Joseph*. (Milwaukee: Bruce Publishing Co., 1951), 208.

February
Image: *Marriage of the Virgin* (c.1670)
Bartolome Esteban Murillo (1617-1682)
© The Wallace Collection, London. Used with permission.

February 1
St. Bernardine of Siena, as quoted in Rosalie Marie Levy, *Joseph the Just Man*. (Derby, New York: Daughters of St. Paul, 1955), 40.

February 2
Blessed Januarius Maria Sarnelli, as quoted in *Favorite Prayers to St. Joseph*. (Charlotte, North Carolina: TAN Books, 1997), 19.

February 3
St. Peter Julian Eymard, *Month of St. Joseph*. (Cleveland, Ohio: Emmanuel Publications, 1948), 2.

February 4
Pope Pius XI, as quoted in Francis L. Filas, SJ, *St. Joseph & Daily Christian Living*. (New York: Macmillan Co., 1959), 195.

February 5
Venerable Pope Pius XII, as quoted in Francis L. Filas, SJ, *St. Joseph & Daily Christian Living*. (New York: Macmillan Co., 1959), 201.

February 6
St. John Paul II, *Redemptoris Custos*, 7.

REFERENCES

February 7
Blessed Pope Pius IX, as quoted in Rosalie Marie Levy, *Joseph the Just Man*. (Derby, New York: Daughters of St. Paul, 1955), 149.

February 8
Pope Pius XI, *Divini Redemptoris,* 81.

February 9
St. Bernardine of Siena, as quoted in Rosalie Marie Levy, *Joseph the Just Man*. (Derby, New York: Daughters of St. Paul, 1955), 39.

February 10
St. Teresa of Avila, as quoted in Rosalie Marie Levy, *Joseph the Just Man*. (Derby, New York: Daughters of St. Paul, 1955), 146.

February 11
Blessed William Joseph Chaminade, *Marian Writings. Vol. 1.* ed. J.B. Armbruster, SM (Dayton, Ohio: Marianist Press, 1980), 235.

February 12
St. John Chrysostom, as quoted in Fr. Richard W. Gilsdorf, *Go to Joseph*. (Green Bay, Wisconsin: Star of the Bay Press, 2009), 21-22.

February 13
St. Bernardine of Siena, as quoted in Francis L. Filas, SJ, *Joseph and Jesus: A Theological Study of Their Relationship*. (Milwaukee: Bruce Publishing Co.), 79.

February 14
St. Francis de Sales, as quoted in Rosalie Marie Levy, *Joseph the Just Man*. (Derby, New York: Daughters of St. Paul, 1955), 129-130.

February 15
Pope Francis, *Meeting with Families in Manila, Philippines* (January 16, 2015).

February 16
St. John Paul II, *Redemptoris Custos,* 8.

February 17
St. Mary Magdalen de Pazzi, as quoted in Antony J. Patrignani, SJ, *A Manual of Practical Devotion to St. Joseph*. (Rockford, Illinois: TAN Books, 1982), 179.

February 18
St. Josemaria Escriva, "A Homily: In Joseph's Workshop," as quoted in Michael D. Griffin, OCD, (ed), *Saint Joseph and the Third Millennium* (Hubertus, Wisconsin: Teresian Charism Press, 1999), 342.

February 19
Blessed Anne Catherine Emmerich, as quoted in Rosalie A. Turton (ed.), *St. Joseph As Seen by Mystics and Historians* (Asbury, New Jersey: 101 Foundation, Inc., 2000), 12.

February 20
Pope Francis, *Meeting with Families in Manila, Philippines* (January 16, 2015).

February 21
St. Peter Damian, as quoted in Antony J. Patrignani, SJ, *A Manual of Practical Devotion to St. Joseph.* (Rockford, Illinois: TAN Books, 1982), 193.

February 22
St. Peter Julian Eymard, as quoted in Rosalie A. Turton (ed.), *St. Joseph As Seen by Mystics and Historians.* (Asbury, New Jersey: 101 Foundation, Inc., 2000), 107.

February 23
Blessed William Joseph Chaminade, *Marian Writings. Vol. 1.* ed. J.B. Armbruster, SM (Dayton, Ohio: Marianist Press, 1980), 112.

February 24
St. Joseph Marello, as quoted in Larry Toschi, OSJ, *St. Joseph in the Lives of Two Blesseds of the Church: Blessed Junipero Serra and Blessed Joseph Marello.* (Santa Cruz, California: Guardian of the Redeemer Books, 1994), 173.

February 25
St. Bernard of Clairvaux, as quoted in Rosalie Marie Levy, *Joseph the Just Man.* (Derby, New York: Daughters of St. Paul, 1955), 42.

February 26
St. Alphonsus Liguori, as quoted in Rev. Nicholas O'Rafferty, *Discourses on St. Joseph.* (Milwaukee: Bruce Publishing Co., 1951), 237.

February 27
St. Thomas Aquinas, as quoted in Fr. Richard W. Gilsdorf, *Go to Joseph.* (Green Bay, Wisconsin: Star of the Bay Press, 2009), 29.

February 28
St. Peter Julian Eymard, as quoted in Rosalie A. Turton (ed.), *St. Joseph As Seen by Mystics and Historians* (Asbury, New Jersey: 101 Foundation, Inc., 2000), 108.

February 29
St. Bernard of Clairvaux, as quoted in Ignace de la Potterie, SJ, *Mary in the Mystery of the Covenant.* (Staten Island, New York: Alba House, 1992), 64.

REFERENCES

March
Image: *St. Joseph Carrying the Child Jesus on the Left Arm*
Pieter van Lint (1609-1690)

March 1
Pope Benedict XV, *Bonum Sane,* as quoted in Francis L. Filas, SJ, *St. Joseph & Daily Christian Living.* (New York: Macmillan Co., 1959), 193.
March 2
St. John Paul II, *Redemptoris Custos,* 8.
March 3
St. Josemaria Escriva, "A Homily: In Joseph's Workshop," as quoted in Michael D. Griffin, OCD, (ed), *Saint Joseph and the Third Millennium.* (Hubertus, Wisconsin: Teresian Charism Press, 1999), 343.
March 4
St. Bernard of Clairvaux, as quoted in Fr. Richard W. Gilsdorf, *Go to Joseph.* (Green Bay, Wisconsin: Star of the Bay Press, 2009), 29.
March 5
St. Clement Mary Hofbauer, as quoted in Rosalie Marie Levy, *Joseph the Just Man.* (Derby, New York: Daughters of St. Paul, 1955), 250.
March 6
St. Madaleine Sophie Barat, as quoted in Rosalie Marie Levy, *Joseph the Just Man.* (Derby, New York: Daughters of St. Paul, 1955), 147-148.
March 7
St. Alphonsus Liguori, as quoted in Rev. Nicholas O'Rafferty, *Discourses on St. Joseph.* (Milwaukee: Bruce Publishing Co., 1951), 236.
March 8
St. John Paul II, as quoted in Domenic de Domenico, OP, *True Devotion to St. Joseph and the Church.* (New Hope, Kentucky: New Hope Publications, 2003), 167.
March 9
St. Francis de Sales, as quoted in Andrew Doze, *Saint Joseph: Shadow of the Father.* trans. Florestine Audett, RJM. (Staten Island, New York: Alba House, 1992), 56.
March 10
St. Alphonsus Liguori, as quoted in Andrew Doze, *Saint Joseph: Shadow of the Father.* trans. Florestine Audett, RJM. (Staten Island, New York: Alba House, 1992), 19-20.

March 11
St. Madaleine Sophie Barat, as quoted in Rosalie Marie Levy, *Joseph the Just Man*. (Derby, New York: Daughters of St. Paul, 1955), 147-148.

March 12
St. Francis de Sales, as quoted in Francis L. Filas, SJ, *Joseph and Jesus: A Theological Study of Their Relationship*. (Milwaukee: Bruce Publishing Co.), 99.

March 13
Blessed Gabriele Allegra, *Mary's Immaculate Heart: A Way to God*. (Chicago, Illinois: Franciscan Herald Press, 1983), 55.

March 14
St. Augustine, as quoted in Fr. Richard W. Gilsdorf, *Go to Joseph*. (Green Bay, Wisconsin: Star of the Bay Press, 2009), 36.

March 15
St. Clement Mary Hofbauer, as quoted in Rosalie Marie Levy, *Joseph the Just Man*. (Derby, New York: Daughters of St. Paul, 1955), 250.

March 16
St. John Paul II, *Redemptoris Custos*, 20.

March 17
Blessed Pope Pius IX, *Quemadmodum Deus* (December 8, 1870).

March 18
St. Jerome, as quoted in Rev. Nicholas O'Rafferty, *Discourses on St. Joseph*. (Milwaukee: Bruce Publishing Co., 1951), 37.

March 19
St. Teresa of Avila, as quoted in Rev. Nicholas O'Rafferty, *Discourses on St. Joseph*. (Milwaukee: Bruce Publishing Co., 1951), 209-210.

March 20
St. Peter Julian Eymard, *Month of St. Joseph*. (Cleveland, Ohio: Emmanuel Publications, 1948), 51.

March 21
Catechism of the Catholic Church, par. 497.

March 22
St. Francis de Sales, as quoted in Rev. Nicholas O'Rafferty, *Discourses on St. Joseph*. (Milwaukee: Bruce Publishing Co., 1951), 38.

March 23
St. John Paul II, *Redemptoris Custos*, 8.

March 24

St. Joseph Marello, as quoted in Larry Toschi, OSJ, *St. Joseph in the Lives of Two Blesseds of the Church: Blessed Junipero Serra and Blessed Joseph Marello.* (Santa Cruz, California: Guardian of the Redeemer Books, 1994), 78.

March 25

St. John Paul II, *Redemptoris Custos,* 5.

March 26

Pope Francis, as quoted in *Magnificat*, May 2014, Vol. 16, No. 3. Pg. 31.

March 27

St. Jerome, as quoted in Francis L. Filas, SJ, *St. Joseph & Daily Christian Living.* (New York: Macmillan Co., 1959), 86.

March 28

Venerable Pope Pius XII, as quoted in Francis L. Filas, SJ, *St. Joseph & Daily Christian Living.* (New York: Macmillan Co., 1959), 202.

March 29

St. John Paul II, *Redemptoris Custos,* 20.

March 30

St. Josemaria Escriva, "A Homily: In Joseph's Workshop," as quoted in Michael D. Griffin, OCD, (ed), *Saint Joseph and the Third Millennium* (Hubertus, Wisconsin: Teresian Charism Press, 1999), 344.

March 31

Blessed Anne Catherine Emmerich, as quoted in Rosalie A. Turton (ed.), *St. Joseph As Seen by Mystics and Historians* (Asbury, New Jersey: 101 Foundation, Inc., 2000), 344.

April

Image: *San José con el Niño Jesús*
Vicente Lopez y Portada (1772-1850)
(Museo Lázaro Galdiano)

April 1

Blessed William Joseph Chaminade, *Marian Writings. Vol. 1.* ed. J.B. Armbruster, SM (Dayton, Ohio: Marianist Press, 1980), 234.

April 2

St. John Paul II, *Redemptoris Custos,* 16.

April 3
St. Jerome, as quoted in Francis L. Filas, SJ, *Joseph and Jesus: A Theological Study of Their Relationship*. (Milwaukee: Bruce Publishing Co.), 34-35.

April 4
Pope Francis, *Meeting with Families in Manila, Philippines* (January 16, 2015).

April 5
Venerable Pope Pius XII, as quoted in Francis L. Filas, SJ, *St. Joseph & Daily Christian Living*. (New York: Macmillan Co., 1959), 201.

April 6
St. Peter Julian Eymard, *Month of St. Joseph*. (Cleveland, Ohio: Emmanuel Publications, 1948), 106.

April 7
St. Bernardine of Siena, as quoted in Rev. Nicholas O'Rafferty, *Discourses on St. Joseph*. (Milwaukee: Bruce Publishing Co., 1951), 191.

April 8
St. Josemaria Escriva, "A Homily: In Joseph's Workshop," as quoted in Michael D. Griffin, OCD, (ed), *Saint Joseph and the Third Millennium* (Hubertus, Wisconsin: Teresian Charism Press, 1999), 357.

April 9
St. Thomas Aquinas, as quoted in Francis L. Filas, SJ, *Joseph and Jesus: A Theological Study of Their Relationship*. (Milwaukee: Bruce Publishing Co.), 73.

April 10
St. Peter Damian, as quoted in Fr. Richard W. Gilsdorf, *Go to Joseph*. (Green Bay, Wisconsin: Star of the Bay Press, 2009), 37.

April 11
St. Bernardine of Siena, as quoted in Francis L. Filas, SJ, *Joseph and Jesus: A Theological Study of Their Relationship*. (Milwaukee: Bruce Publishing Co.), 79.

April 12
Blessed William Joseph Chaminade, *Marian Writings. Vol. 1*. ed. J.B. Armbruster, SM (Dayton, Ohio: Marianist Press, 1980), 121.

April 13
Blessed Pope Pius IX, *Acta Sanctae Sedis*, 6, 324.

April 14
St. Maximilian Kolbe, *The Writings of St. Maximilian Kolbe*. Vol. II. (Lugano, Switzerland: Nerbini International, 2016), 1604.

April 15
St. Bernardine of Siena, as quoted in Francis L. Filas, SJ, *Joseph and Jesus: A Theological Study of Their Relationship.* (Milwaukee: Bruce Publishing Co.), 79.

April 16
St. Bernadette Soubirous, as quoted in Andrew Doze, *Saint Joseph: Shadow of the Father.* trans. Florestine Audett, RJM. (Staten Island, New York: Alba House, 1992), 68.

April 17
St. Peter Julian Eymard, *Month of St. Joseph.* (Cleveland, Ohio: Emmanuel Publications, 1948), 84.

April 18
St. Alphonsus Liguori, as quoted in Rosalie Marie Levy, *Joseph the Just Man.* (Derby, New York: Daughters of St. Paul, 1955), 144.

April 19
St. Peter Julian Eymard, *Month of St. Joseph.* (Cleveland, Ohio: Emmanuel Publications, 1948), 106.

April 20
St. Joseph Marello, as quoted in Larry Toschi, OSJ, *St. Joseph in the Lives of Two Blesseds of the Church: Blessed Junipero Serra and Blessed Joseph Marello.* (Santa Cruz, California: Guardian of the Redeemer Books, 1994), 81.

April 21
St. Alphonsus Liguori, as quoted in Rev. Nicholas O'Rafferty, *Discourses on St. Joseph.* (Milwaukee: Bruce Publishing Co., 1951), 236.

April 22
St. Francis de Sales, as quoted in Rosalie Marie Levy, *Joseph the Just Man.* (Derby, New York: Daughters of St. Paul, 1955), 143.

April 23
Pope Leo XIII, as quoted in Francis L. Filas, *Joseph: The Man Closest to Jesus.* (Boston, Massachusetts: Daughters of St. Paul, 1962), 102.

April 24
St. Lawrence of Brindisi, *Opera Omnia: Feastday Sermons.* trans. Vernon Wagner, OFM Cap (Delhi, India: Media House, 2007), 535.

April 25
St. John Paul II, *Redemptoris Custos,* 8.

April 26
Blessed Hyacinth Marie Cormier, as quoted in Francis Xavier Lasance, *With God: A Book of Prayers and Reflections.* (New York: Benziger Bros., 1911), 750-751.

April 27
St. Albert the Great, as quoted in Fr. Richard W. Gilsdorf, *Go to Joseph.* (Green Bay, Wisconsin: Star of the Bay Press, 2009), 37.

April 28
St. Louis de Montfort, *God Alone: The Collected Writings of St. Louis de Montfort.* (Bay Shore, New York: Montfort Publications, 1995), 241

April 29
Venerable Pope Pius XII, as quoted in Francis L. Filas, SJ, *St. Joseph & Daily Christian Living.* (New York: Macmillan Co., 1959), 202.

April 30
Blessed Gabriele Allegra, *Mary's Immaculate Heart: A Way to God.* (Chicago, Illinois: Franciscan Herald Press, 1983), 55.

May
Image: *St. Joseph and the Christ Child* (1648)
Francisco de Herrera the Elder (1576-1656)
Museo Lázaro Galdiano, Madrid

May 1
Pope Francis, *General Audience* (May 1, 2013).

May 2
Pope Benedict XVI (Joseph Cardinal Ratzinger) & Hans Urs von Balthasar, *Mary: The Church at the Source.* trans. Adrian Walker (San Francisco: Ignatius Press, 2005), 88.

May 3
Ven. Fulton J. Sheen, *The World's First Love: Mary, Mother of God.* (San Francisco: Ignatius Press, 1996), 93.

May 4
St. Cyril of Jerusalem, as quoted in Fr. Richard W. Gilsdorf, *Go to Joseph.* (Green Bay, Wisconsin: Star of the Bay Press, 2009), 57.

May 5
Venerable Pope Pius XII, as quoted in Francis L. Filas, SJ, *St. Joseph & Daily Christian Living.* (New York: Macmillan Co., 1959), 197.

May 6
St. Jerome, as quoted in Francis L. Filas, SJ, *Joseph and Jesus: A Theological Study of Their Relationship*. (Milwaukee: Bruce Publishing Co.), 35.

May 7
St. Peter Julian Eymard, *Month of St. Joseph*. (Cleveland, Ohio: Emmanuel Publications, 1948), 84.

May 8
St. Teresa of Avila, as quoted in Antony J. Patrignani, SJ, *A Manual of Practical Devotion to St. Joseph*. (Rockford, Illinois: TAN Books, 1982), 223.

May 9
St. Bernard of Clairvaux, as quoted in Devin Schadt, *Joseph's Way: The Call to Fatherly Greatness*. (San Francisco, California: Ignatius Press, 2013), 266.

May 10
St. Thomas Aquinas, as quoted in Devin Schadt, *Joseph's Way: The Call to Fatherly Greatness*. (San Francisco, California: Ignatius Press, 2013), 267.

May 11
Pope Leo XIII, as quoted in Fr. Richard W. Gilsdorf, *Go to Joseph*. (Green Bay, Wisconsin: Star of the Bay Press, 2009), 111.

May 12
St. Francis de Sales, as quoted in Francis L. Filas, SJ, *Joseph and Jesus: A Theological Study of Their Relationship*. (Milwaukee: Bruce Publishing Co.), 100.

May 13
Ven. Fulton J. Sheen, *The World's First Love: Mary, Mother of God*. (San Francisco: Ignatius Press, 1996), 93.

May 14
Pope Leo XIII, as quoted in Francis L. Filas, SJ, *St. Joseph & Daily Christian Living*. (New York: Macmillan Co., 1959), 52.

May 15
Blessed Gabriele Allegra, *Mary's Immaculate Heart: A Way to God*. (Chicago, Illinois: Franciscan Herald Press, 1983), 55.

May 16
Venerable Pope Pius XII, as quoted in Francis L. Filas, SJ, *St. Joseph & Daily Christian Living*. (New York: Macmillan Co., 1959), 200.

May 17
St. Lawrence of Brindisi, *Opera Omnia: Feastday Sermons*. trans. Vernon Wagner, OFM Cap (Delhi, India: Media House, 2007), 539.

May 18
St. Stanislaus Papczynski, *St. Stanislaus Papczynski: The Life and Writings of the Marians' Founder.* (Stockbridge, Massachusetts: Marian Press, 2016), 85-86.

May 19
St. Francis de Sales, as quoted in Rev. Nicholas O'Rafferty, *Discourses on St. Joseph.* (Milwaukee: Bruce Publishing Co., 1951), 38.

May 20
St. Bernardine of Siena, as quoted in Maria Cecilia Baij, OSB, *The Life of St. Joseph.* (Asbury, New Jersey: 101 Foundation, Inc., 1996), 396.

May 21
Blessed Hyacinth Marie Cormier, as quoted in Francis Xavier Lasance, *With God: A Book of Prayers and Reflections.* (New York: Benziger Bros., 1911), 750-751.

May 22
Pope Leo XIII, as quoted in Rev. Nicholas O'Rafferty, *Discourses on St. Joseph.* (Milwaukee: Bruce Publishing Co., 1951), 235-236.

May 23
St. Francis de Sales, as quoted in Rosalie Marie Levy, *Joseph the Just Man.* (Derby, New York: Daughters of St. Paul, 1955), 129-130.

May 24
St. Teresa of Avila, as quoted in Rosalie Marie Levy, *Joseph the Just Man.* (Derby, New York: Daughters of St. Paul, 1955), 147.

May 25
St. Madaleine Sophie Barat, as quoted in Rosalie Marie Levy, *Joseph the Just Man.* (Derby, New York: Daughters of St. Paul, 1955), 147-148.

May 26
St. Mary Magdalen de Pazzi, as quoted in Antony J. Patrignani, SJ, *A Manual of Practical Devotion to St. Joseph.* (Rockford, Illinois: TAN Books, 1982), 179.

May 27
Blessed Januarius Maria Sarnelli, as quoted in *Favorite Prayers to St. Joseph.* (Charlotte, North Carolina: TAN Books, 1997), 20.

May 28
Pope Leo XIII, *Quamquam Pluries,* 3.

May 29
St. Francis de Sales, as quoted in Rev. Nicholas O'Rafferty, *Discourses on St. Joseph.* (Milwaukee: Bruce Publishing Co., 1951), 203.

May 30
St. Joseph Marello, as quoted in Larry Toschi, OSJ, *Husband, Father, Worker: Questions and Answers about St. Joseph.* (Liguori, MO: Liguori, 2012), 70.

May 31
St. Peter Julian Eymard, *Month of St. Joseph.* (Cleveland, Ohio: Emmanuel Publications, 1948), 106.

June
Image: *The Dream of St. Joseph* (c. 1773). Anton Raphael Mengs (1728-1779). © KHM-Museumsverbrand.

June 1
St. Bernardine of Siena, as quoted in Rev. Nicholas O'Rafferty, *Discourses on St. Joseph.* (Milwaukee: Bruce Publishing Co., 1951), 191.

June 2
Ven. Mary of Agreda, as quoted in Rosalie Marie Levy, *Joseph the Just Man.* (Derby, New York: Daughters of St. Paul, 1955), 85.

June 3
Blessed Gabriele Allegra, *Mary's Immaculate Heart: A Way to God.* (Chicago, Illinois: Franciscan Herald Press, 1983), 55.

June 4
St. Ambrose, as quoted in Rev. Nicholas O'Rafferty, *Discourses on St. Joseph.* (Milwaukee: Bruce Publishing Co., 1951), 206.

June 5
Blessed Pope Paul VI, *Discourse* (March 19, 1969): *Insegnamenti,* VII (1969), p. 1268.

June 6
St. Teresa of Avila, as quoted in Rev. Nicholas O'Rafferty, *Discourses on St. Joseph.* (Milwaukee: Bruce Publishing Co., 1951), 209.

June 7
St. Leonard of Port Maurice, as quoted in Andrew Doze, *Saint Joseph: Shadow of the Father.* trans. Florestine Audett, RJM. (Staten Island, New York: Alba House, 1992), 18.

June 8
St. Alphonsus Liguori, as quoted in Rev. Nicholas O'Rafferty, *Discourses on St. Joseph.* (Milwaukee: Bruce Publishing Co., 1951), 236.

June 9
St. Ephrem the Syrian, as quoted in Rosalie Marie Levy, *Joseph the Just Man.* (Derby, New York: Daughters of St. Paul, 1955), 152.

June 10
St. Francis de Sales, as quoted in Rosalie Marie Levy, *Joseph the Just Man.* (Derby, New York: Daughters of St. Paul, 1955), 142.

June 11
St. Lawrence of Brindisi, *Opera Omnia: Feastday Sermons.* trans. Vernon Wagner, OFM Cap (Delhi, India: Media House, 2007), 539.

June 12
St. Peter Julian Eymard, *Month of St. Joseph.* (Cleveland, Ohio: Emmanuel Publications, 1948), 23.

June 13
St. Joseph Marello, as quoted in Larry Toschi, OSJ, *Husband, Father, Worker: Questions and Answers about St. Joseph.* (Liguori, MO: Liguori, 2012), 71.

June 14
St. Teresa of Avila, as quoted in Rosalie Marie Levy, *Joseph, the Just Man.* (Derby, New York: Daughters of St. Paul, 1955), 146.

June 15
St. Alphonsus Liguori, as quoted in Andrew Doze, *Saint Joseph: Shadow of the Father.* trans. Florestine Audett, RJM (Staten Island, New York: Alba House, 1992), 19.

June 16
St. Alphonsus Liguori, as quoted in Andrew Doze, *Saint Joseph: Shadow of the Father.* trans. Florestine Audett, RJM (Staten Island, New York: Alba House, 1992), 19-20.

June 17
St. Lawrence of Brindisi, *Opera Omnia: Feastday Sermons.* trans. Vernon Wagner, OFM Cap (Delhi, India: Media House, 2007), 538.

June 18
St. Bernardine of Siena, as quoted in Rosalie Marie Levy, *Joseph, the Just Man.* (Derby, New York: Daughters of St. Paul, 1955), 144-145.

June 19
Blessed William Joseph Chaminade, *Marian Writings. Vol. 1.* ed. J.B. Armbruster, SM (Dayton, Ohio: Marianist Press, 1980), 112.

June 20

Ven. Fulton J. Sheen, *The World's First Love: Mary, Mother of God*. (San Francisco: Ignatius Press, 1996), 245.

June 21

St. Alphonsus Liguori, as quoted in Rev. Nicholas O'Rafferty, *Discourses on St. Joseph*. (Milwaukee: Bruce Publishing Co., 1951), 207.

June 22

St. Peter Julian Eymard, *Month of St. Joseph*. (Cleveland, Ohio: Emmanuel Publications, 1948), 23.

June 23

Pope Pius XI, as quoted in Francis L. Filas, SJ, *St. Joseph & Daily Christian Living*. (New York: Macmillan Co., 1959), 194.

June 24

St. Lawrence of Brindisi, *Opera Omnia: Feastday Sermons*. trans. Vernon Wagner, OFM Cap (Delhi, India: Media House, 2007), 538.

June 25

Venerable Pope Pius XII, as quoted in Francis L. Filas, SJ, *St. Joseph & Daily Christian Living*. (New York: Macmillan Co., 1959), 200.

June 26

St. Josemaría Escrivá, as quoted in Federico Suarez, *Joseph of Nazareth*. (Oxford: Scepter Press, 1984), 19.

June 27

St. André Bessette, as quoted in Henri-Paul Bergeron, CSC, *Brother Andre: The Wonder Man of Mount Royal*. trans. Rev. Real Boudreau, CSC. (Montreal: Saint Joseph Oratory, 1997), 80.

June 28

St. Irenaeus of Lyons, as quoted in Antony J. Patrignani, SJ, *A Manual of Practical Devotion to St. Joseph*. (Rockford, Illinois: TAN Books, 1982), 216.

June 29

St. Alphonsus Liguori, as quoted in Rosalie Marie Levy, *Joseph the Just Man*. (Derby, New York: Daughters of St. Paul, 1955), 143.

June 30

Blessed Januarius Maria Sarnelli, as quoted in *Favorite Prayers to St. Joseph*. (Charlotte, North Carolina: TAN Books, 1997), 20.

July
Image: *The Holy Family with a Bird* (c.1650)
Bartolome Esteban Murillo (1617-1682)
© Prado, Madrid, Spain/Bridgeman Images

July 1
Blessed Gabriele Allegra, *Mary's Immaculate Heart: A Way to God.* (Chicago, Illinois: Franciscan Herald Press, 1983), 55.

July 2
St. Bernard of Clairvaux, as quoted in Rosalie Marie Levy, *Joseph the Just Man.* (Derby, New York: Daughters of St. Paul, 1955), 42-43.

July 3
St. John Paul II, *Redemptoris Custos,* 22.

July 4
Blessed Pope Paul VI, *Discourse* (March 19, 1969): *Insegnamenti,* VII (1969), p. 1268.

July 5
Blessed William Joseph Chaminade, *Marian Writings. Vol. 1.* ed. J.B. Armbruster, SM (Dayton, Ohio: Marianist Press, 1980), 114.

July 6
Pope Leo XIII, *Quamquam Pluries,* 3.

July 7
St. Francis de Sales, as quoted in Rev. Nicholas O'Rafferty, *Discourses on St. Joseph.* (Milwaukee: Bruce Publishing Co., 1951), 203.

July 8
Pope Leo XIII, *Quamquam Pluries,* 3.

July 9
St. Francis de Sales, as quoted in Rosalie Marie Levy, *Joseph, the Just Man.* (Derby, New York: Daughters of St. Paul, 1955), 140.

July 10
Pope Pius XI, *Divini Redemptoris,* 81.

July 11
Pope Leo XIII, *Quamquam Pluries,* 3.

July 12
St. Mary Magdalen de Pazzi, as quoted in Antony J. Patrignani, SJ, *A Manual of Practical Devotion to St. Joseph.* (Rockford, Illinois: TAN Books, 1982), 179.

REFERENCES

July 13
Blessed William Joseph Chaminade, *Marian Writings. Vol. 1.* ed. J.B. Armbruster, SM (Dayton, Ohio: Marianist Press, 1980), 112.

July 14
Pope Leo XIII, *Quamquam Pluries,* 3.

July 15
St. Bonaventure, as quoted in Antony J. Patrignani, SJ, *A Manual of Practical Devotion to St. Joseph.* (Rockford, Illinois: TAN Books, 1982), 206.

July 16
St. Bernardine of Siena, as quoted in Rosalie Marie Levy, *Joseph, the Just Man.* (Derby, New York: Daughters of St. Paul, 1955), 144-145.

July 17
Ven. Mary of Agreda, as quoted in *Favorite Prayers to St. Joseph.* (Charlotte, North Carolina: TAN Books, 1997), 14.

July 18
Blessed William Joseph Chaminade, *Marian Writings. Vol. 1.* ed. J.B. Armbruster, SM (Dayton, Ohio: Marianist Press, 1980), 117.

July 19
St. Francis de Sales, as quoted in Rosalie Marie Levy, *Joseph, the Just Man.* (Derby, New York: Daughters of St. Paul, 1955), 131.

July 20
St. Pope Pius X, as quoted in Larry Toschi, OSJ, *Husband, Father, Worker: Questions and Answers about St. Joseph.* (Liguori, MO: Liguori, 2012), 108.

July 21
St. Lawrence of Brindisi, *Opera Omnia: Feastday Sermons.* trans. Vernon Wagner, OFM Cap (Delhi, India: Media House, 2007), 535.

July 22
St. Francis de Sales, as quoted in Rosalie Marie Levy, *Joseph, the Just Man.* (Derby, New York: Daughters of St. Paul, 1955), 140.

July 23
St. Bridget of Sweden, as quoted in Antony J. Patrignani, SJ, *A Manual of Practical Devotion to St. Joseph.* (Rockford, Illinois: TAN Books, 1982), 206.

July 24
St. Peter Julian Eymard, as quoted in Rosalie Marie Levy, *Joseph, the Just Man.* (Derby, New York: Daughters of St. Paul, 1955), 149.

July 25
St. Francis de Sales, as quoted in Rosalie Marie Levy, *Joseph, the Just Man.* (Derby, New York: Daughters of St. Paul, 1955), 140.

July 26
Blessed Gabriele Allegra, *Mary's Immaculate Heart: A Way to God.* (Chicago, Illinois: Franciscan Herald Press, 1983), 78.

July 27
Blessed William Joseph Chaminade, *Marian Writings. Vol. 1.* ed. J.B. Armbruster, SM (Dayton, Ohio: Marianist Press, 1980), 121.

July 28
St. Francis de Sales, as quoted in Rosalie Marie Levy, *Joseph the Just Man.* (Derby, New York: Daughters of St. Paul, 1955), 142.

July 29
Blessed Pope Pius IX, *Inclytum Patriarcham* (July 7, 1871)

July 30
St. Teresa of Avila, as quoted in Rev. Nicholas O'Rafferty, *Discourses on St. Joseph.* (Milwaukee: Bruce Publishing Co., 1951), 209.

July 31
Pope Benedict XV, *Bonum Sane,* as quoted in Francis L. Filas, SJ, *St. Joseph & Daily Christian Living.* (New York: Macmillan Co., 1959), 192.

August
Image: *San José, Refugio de los Agonizantes.* Miguel Cabrera (1695-1768) Museo Nacional del Virreinato, Tepozotlán, Edo. de México.

August 1
St. Alphonsus Liguori, as quoted in Maria Cecilia Baij, OSB, *The Life of St. Joseph.* (Asbury, New Jersey: 101 Foundation, Inc., 1996), 416.

August 2
St. Peter Julian Eymard, *Month of St. Joseph.* (Cleveland, Ohio: Emmanuel Publications, 1948), 8.

August 3
St. John Paul II, *Redemptoris Custos,* 32.

August 4
Pope Leo XIII, as quoted in Rev. Nicholas O'Rafferty, *Discourses on St. Joseph.* (Milwaukee: Bruce Publishing Co., 1951), 169.

August 5
Blessed Pope Pius IX, *Quemadmodum Deus* (December 8, 1870).
August 6
St. Francis de Sales, as quoted in Rosalie Marie Levy, *Joseph, the Just Man*. (Derby, New York: Daughters of St. Paul, 1955), 137.
August 7
St. Lawrence of Brindisi, *Opera Omnia: Feastday Sermons*. trans. Vernon Wagner, OFM Cap (Delhi, India: Media House, 2007), 538.
August 8
St. Josemaria Escriva, "A Homily: In Joseph's Workshop," as quoted in Michael D. Griffin, OCD, (ed), *Saint Joseph and the Third Millennium*. (Hubertus, Wisconsin: Teresian Charism Press, 1999), 358.
August 9
Blessed William Joseph Chaminade, *Marian Writings. Vol. 1*. ed. J.B. Armbruster, SM (Dayton, Ohio: Marianist Press, 1980), 223-224.
August 10
Pope Pius XI, *Divini Redemptoris,* 81.
August 11
St. John Paul II, as quoted in Domenic de Domenico, OP, *True Devotion to St. Joseph and the Church*. (New Hope, Kentucky: New Hope Publications, 2003), 167.
August 12
St. Francis de Sales, as quoted in Rosalie Marie Levy, *Joseph, the Just Man*. (Derby, New York: Daughters of St. Paul, 1955), 138.
August 13
St. Thomas Aquinas, as quoted in Rev. Nicholas O'Rafferty, *Discourses on St. Joseph*. (Milwaukee: Bruce Publishing Co., 1951), 208.
August 14
St. Maximilian Kolbe, *The Writings of St. Maximilian Kolbe*. Vol. II. (Lugano, Switzerland: Nerbini International, 2016), 1624.
August 15
St. Francis de Sales, as quoted in Andrew Doze, *Saint Joseph: Shadow of the Father*. trans. Florestine Audett, RJM (Staten Island, New York: Alba House, 1992), 56.
August 16
Blessed William Joseph Chaminade, *Marian Writings. Vol. 1*. ed. J.B. Armbruster, SM (Dayton, Ohio: Marianist Press, 1980), 235.

August 17
St. Alphonsus Liguori, as quoted in Maria Cecilia Baij, OSB, *The Life of St. Joseph.* (Asbury, New Jersey: 101 Foundation, Inc., 1996), 416.

August 18
Blessed William Joseph Chaminade, *Marian Writings. Vol. 1.* ed. J.B. Armbruster, SM (Dayton, Ohio: Marianist Press, 1980), 224.

August 19
St. Josemaria Escriva, "A Homily: In Joseph's Workshop," as quoted in Michael D. Griffin, OCD, (ed), *Saint Joseph and the Third Millennium* (Hubertus, Wisconsin: Teresian Charism Press, 1999), 358.

August 20
St. Bernard of Clairvaux, as quoted in Rosalie Marie Levy, *Joseph, the Just Man.* (Derby, New York: Daughters of St. Paul, 1955), 27-28.

August 21
Pope St. Pius X, as quoted in Rev. Nicholas O'Rafferty, *Discourses on St. Joseph.* (Milwaukee: Bruce Publishing Co., 1951), 49.

August 22
Blessed William Joseph Chaminade, *Marian Writings. Vol. II.* ed. J.B. Armbruster, SM (Dayton, Ohio: Marianist Press, 1980), 52.

August 23
Blessed Pope Pius IX, *Quemadmodum Deus* (December 8, 1870).

August 24
St. Francis de Sales, as quoted in Rosalie Marie Levy, *Joseph, the Just Man.* (Derby, New York: Daughters of St. Paul, 1955), 130-131.

August 25
St. Lawrence of Brindisi, *Opera Omnia: Feastday Sermons.* trans. Vernon Wagner, OFM Cap (Delhi, India: Media House, 2007), 538.

August 26
St. Francis de Sales, as quoted in Rev. Nicholas O'Rafferty, *Discourses on St. Joseph.* (Milwaukee: Bruce Publishing Co., 1951), 203.

August 27
St. Pope John XXIII, as quoted in Fr. Richard W. Gilsdorf, *Go to Joseph.* (Green Bay, Wisconsin: Star of the Bay Press, 2009), 116

August 28
St. Augustine, as quoted in Francis L. Filas, SJ, *Joseph and Jesus: A Theological Study of Their Relationship.* (Milwaukee: Bruce Publishing Co.), 40.

August 29
Blessed John Henry Newman, as quoted in Maria Cecilia Baij, OSB, *The Life of St. Joseph.* (Asbury, New Jersey: 101 Foundation, Inc., 1996), 422.
August 30
Blessed William Joseph Chaminade, *Marian Writings. Vol. I.* ed. J.B. Armbruster, SM (Dayton, Ohio: Marianist Press, 1980), 226.
August 31
St. John Paul II, *Redemptoris Custos,* 27.

September
Image: *San José, Refugio de los Agonizantes*
Miguel Cabrera (1695-1768)
Museo Nacional del Virreinato, Tepozotlán, Edo. de México.

September 1
Blessed Pope Pius IX, *Quemadmodum Deus* (December 8, 1870).
September 2
St. Peter Julian Eymard, as quoted in Rosalie A. Turton (ed.), *St. Joseph As Seen by Mystics and Historians.* (Asbury, New Jersey: 101 Foundation, Inc., 2000), 317.
September 3
St. Pope Pius X, as quoted in Blessed Gabriele Allegra, *Mary's Immaculate Heart: A Way to God.* (Chicago, Illinois: Franciscan Herald Press, 1983), 138.
September 4
Blessed William Joseph Chaminade, *Marian Writings. Vol. II.* ed. J.B. Armbruster, SM (Dayton, Ohio: Marianist Press, 1980), 52.
September 5
Pope Benedict XVI, as quoted in Fr. Richard W. Gilsdorf, *Go to Joseph.* (Green Bay, Wisconsin: Star of the Bay Press, 2009), 122
September 6
St. Peter Julian Eymard, *Month of St. Joseph.* (Cleveland, Ohio: Emmanuel Publications, 1948), 8.
September 7
Blessed Anne Catherine Emmerich, as quoted in Rosalie A. Turton (ed.), *St. Joseph As Seen by Mystics and Historians.* (Asbury, New Jersey: 101 Foundation, Inc., 2000), 344.

September 8
Venerable Mary of Agreda, as quoted in Rosalie A. Turton (ed.), *St. Joseph As Seen by Mystics and Historians.* (Asbury, New Jersey: 101 Foundation, Inc., 2000), 358.

September 9
St. Peter Julian Eymard, *Month of St. Joseph.* (Cleveland, Ohio: Emmanuel Publications, 1948), 6-7.

September 10
St. Bernardine of Siena, as quoted in Antony J. Patrignani, SJ, *A Manual of Practical Devotion to St. Joseph.* (Rockford, Illinois: TAN Books, 1982), 226.

September 11
Pope Leo XIII, as quoted in Rev. Nicholas O'Rafferty, *Discourses on St. Joseph.* (Milwaukee: Bruce Publishing Co., 1951), 235-236.

September 12
Blessed William Joseph Chaminade, as quoted in Maria Cecilia Baij, OSB, *The Life of St. Joseph.* (Asbury, New Jersey: 101 Foundation, Inc., 1996), 421.

September 13
Blessed William Joseph Chaminade, *Marian Writings. Vol. I.* ed. J.B. Armbruster, SM (Dayton, Ohio: Marianist Press, 1980), 226.

September 14
St. Francis de Sales, as quoted in Rev. Nicholas O'Rafferty, *Discourses on St. Joseph.* (Milwaukee: Bruce Publishing Co., 1951), 203.

September 15
St. Peter Julian Eymard, *Month of St. Joseph.* (Cleveland, Ohio: Emmanuel Publications, 1948), 90.

September 16
St. Bernardine of Siena, as quoted in Francis L. Filas, SJ, *Joseph and Jesus: A Theological Study of Their Relationship.* (Milwaukee: Bruce Publishing Co.), 79.

September 17
Blessed William Joseph Chaminade, *Marian Writings. Vol. 1.* ed. J.B. Armbruster, SM (Dayton, Ohio: Marianist Press, 1980), 236.

September 18
Blessed William Joseph Chaminade, *Marian Writings. Vol. 1.* ed. J.B. Armbruster, SM (Dayton, Ohio: Marianist Press, 1980), 224.

September 19
Blessed James Alberione, *Mary, Queen of Apostles.* (Boston, Massachusetts: Daughters of St. Paul, 1976), 142.

September 20

St. Josemaria Escriva, "A Homily: In Joseph's Workshop," as quoted in Michael D. Griffin, OCD, (ed), *Saint Joseph and the Third Millennium*. (Hubertus, Wisconsin: Teresian Charism Press, 1999), 341-342.

September 21

Blessed William Joseph Chaminade, *Marian Writings. Vol. 1*. ed. J.B. Armbruster, SM (Dayton, Ohio: Marianist Press, 1980), 224.

September 22

Pope Francis, *Meeting with Families in Manila, Philippines*. (January 16, 2015).

September 23

St. Bernadette Soubirous, as quoted in René Laurentin, *Presence of Saint Joseph in the Life of Bernadette of Lourdes*. (Montréal: Oratoire Saint-Joseph, 1998), 4.

September 24

Blessed William Joseph Chaminade, as quoted in *From a Full Heart: Thoughts from Father Chaminade* (North American Center for Marianist Studies, NACMS). Compiled by Francis J. Greiner, SM, (St. Meinard, Indiana: The Grail Press, 1949), entry for March 12.

September 25

Pope Benedict XVI, as quoted in Fr. Richard W. Gilsdorf, *Go to Joseph*. (Green Bay, Wisconsin: Star of the Bay Press, 2009), 127.

September 26

Blessed Pope Paul VI, as quoted in St. John Paul II, *Redemptoris Custos*, 7.

September 27

Pope Pius XI, *Divini Redemptoris*, 81.

September 28

St. Peter Julian Eymard, *Month of St. Joseph*. (Cleveland, Ohio: Emmanuel Publications, 1948), 6-7.

September 29

Pope Francis, *Meeting with Families in Manila, Philippines*. (January 16, 2015).

September 30

St. Jerome, as quoted in Francis L. Filas, SJ, *St. Joseph & Daily Christian Living*. (New York: Macmillan Co., 1959), 71.

October

Image: *Holy Family*
Claudio Coello (1642-1693)
© Szépművészeti Múzeum / Museum of Fine Arts Budapest, 2017,
Photographer: Dénes JÓZSA. Used with permission.

October 1
St. Peter Julian Eymard, *Month of St. Joseph*. (Cleveland, Ohio: Emmanuel Publications, 1948), 41.

October 2
St. Pope John XXIII, as quoted in Francis L. Filas, *Joseph: The Man Closest to Jesus*. (Boston, Massachusetts: Daughters of St. Paul, 1962), 629.

October 3
Pope Benedict XVI, as quoted in Fr. Richard W. Gilsdorf, *Go to Joseph*. (Green Bay, Wisconsin: Star of the Bay Press, 2009), 127-128.

October 4
St. Bernardine of Siena, as quoted in Rosalie Marie Levy, *Joseph, the Just Man*. (Derby, New York: Daughters of St. Paul, 1955), 245.

October 5
St. Faustina Kowalska, *Diary: Divine Mercy in My Soul*. (Stockbridge, Massachusetts: Marian Press, 2002), par. 1203.

October 6
Venerable Pope Pius XII, as quoted in Francis L. Filas, SJ, *St. Joseph & Daily Christian Living*. (New York: Macmillan Co., 1959), 200.

October 7
Blessed Gabriele Allegra, *Mary's Immaculate Heart: A Way to God*. (Chicago, Illinois: Franciscan Herald Press, 1983), 72.

October 8
St. Thomas Aquinas, as quoted in Francis L. Filas, *Joseph: The Man Closest to Jesus*. (Boston, Massachusetts: Daughters of St. Paul, 1962), 101.

October 9
Blessed John Henry Newman, as quoted in Maria Cecilia Baij, OSB, *The Life of St. Joseph*. (Asbury, New Jersey: 101 Foundation, Inc., 1996), 422.

October 10
St. John Paul II, *Redemptoris Custos*, 27.

REFERENCES

October 11
St. John Paul II, *Redemptoris Custos,* 6.

October 12
Blessed Gabriele Allegra, *Mary's Immaculate Heart: A Way to God.* (Chicago, Illinois: Franciscan Herald Press, 1983), 55.

October 13
Servant of God Lucia Dos Santos, as quoted in *Favorite Prayers to St. Joseph.* (Charlotte, North Carolina: TAN Books, 1997), 28.

October 14
Blessed William Joseph Chaminade, *The Chaminade Legacy.* Monograph Series. Document no. 53, Volume 2. trans. Joseph Stefanelli, SM (Dayton, Ohio: NACMS, 2008), 412.

October 15
St. Teresa of Avila, as quoted in Rosalie Marie Levy, *Joseph, the Just Man.* (Derby, New York: Daughters of St. Paul, 1955), 145.

October 16
Blessed William Joseph Chaminade, *Marian Writings. Vol. 1.* ed. J.B. Armbruster, SM (Dayton, Ohio: Marianist Press, 1980), 227-228.

October 17
Pope Benedict XVI, as quoted in Fr. Richard W. Gilsdorf, *Go to Joseph.* (Green Bay, Wisconsin: Star of the Bay Press, 2009), 128.

October 18
Blessed William Joseph Chaminade, *Marian Writings. Vol. 1.* ed. J.B. Armbruster, SM (Dayton, Ohio: Marianist Press, 1980), 228.

October 19
Pope Benedict XVI, as quoted in Fr. Richard W. Gilsdorf, *Go to Joseph.* (Green Bay, Wisconsin: Star of the Bay Press, 2009), 127.

October 20
Blessed William Joseph Chaminade, *Marian Writings. Vol. II.* ed. J.B. Armbruster, SM (Dayton, Ohio: Marianist Press, 1980), 52.

October 21
St. Peter Julian Eymard, *Month of St. Joseph.* (Cleveland, Ohio: Emmanuel Publications, 1948), 2.

October 22
St. John Paul II, *Redemptoris Custos,* 30.

October 23
Blessed Gabriele Allegra, *Mary's Immaculate Heart: A Way to God.* (Chicago, Illinois: Franciscan Herald Press, 1983), 56.

October 24
St. Anthony Mary Claret, *The Golden Key to Heaven.* (Buffalo, New York: Immaculate Heart Publications, 1955), 132.

October 25
St. Teresa of Avila, as quoted in Rev. Nicholas O'Rafferty, *Discourses on St. Joseph.* (Milwaukee: Bruce Publishing Co., 1951), 209.

October 26
St. Augustine, as quoted in Francis L. Filas, SJ, *Joseph and Jesus: A Theological Study of Their Relationship.* (Milwaukee: Bruce Publishing Co.), 45.

October 27
St. Francis de Sales, as quoted in Domenic de Domenico, OP, *True Devotion to St. Joseph and the Church.* (New Hope, Kentucky: New Hope Publications, 2003), 22.

October 28
St. Luigi Guanella, as quoted in *L'Osservatore Romano* (March 16, 2011), 9.

October 29
St. Francis de Sales, as quoted in Maria Cecilia Baij, OSB, *The Life of St. Joseph.* (Asbury, New Jersey: 101 Foundation, Inc., 1996), 388.

October 30
Venerable Pops Pius XII, as quoted in Francis L. Filas, SJ, *St. Joseph & Daily Christian Living.* (New York: Macmillan Co., 1959), 203.

October 31
Ven. Fulton J. Sheen, *The World's First Love: Mary, Mother of God.* (San Francisco: Ignatius Press, 1996), 202.

November
Image: *Death of St. Joseph* (c.1712)
Giuseppe Maria Crespi (1665-1747)
© State Hermitage Museum, St. Petersburg, Russia / Bridgeman Images

November 1
Blessed William Joseph Chaminade, *Marian Writings. Vol. 1.* ed. J.B. Armbruster, SM (Dayton, Ohio: Marianist Press, 1980), 236.

REFERENCES

November 2
St. Bernardine of Siena, as quoted in Blessed William Joseph Chaminade, *The Chaminade Legacy*. Monograph Series. Document no. 53, Volume 2. trans. Joseph Stefanelli, SM (Dayton, Ohio: NACMS, 2008), 414-415.

November 3
Venerable Pope Pius XII, as quoted in Francis L. Filas, SJ, *St. Joseph & Daily Christian Living*. (New York: Macmillan Co., 1959), 201.

November 4
St. Francis de Sales, as quoted in Rosalie Marie Levy, *Joseph, the Just Man*. (Derby, New York: Daughters of St. Paul, 1955), 141.

November 5
St. Peter Julian Eymard, *Month of St. Joseph*. (Cleveland, Ohio: Emmanuel Publications, 1948), 101.

November 6
Pope Leo XIII, as quoted in Rev. Nicholas O'Rafferty, *Discourses on St. Joseph*. (Milwaukee: Bruce Publishing Co., 1951), 168-169.

November 7
St. John Paul II, *Redemptoris Custos*, 27.

November 8
Pope Leo XIII, as quoted in Francis L. Filas, SJ, *Joseph and Jesus: A Theological Study of Their Relationship*. (Milwaukee: Bruce Publishing Co.), 117.

November 9
St. Bernard of Clairvaux, as quoted in Rosalie Marie Levy, *Joseph the Just Man*. (Derby, New York: Daughters of St. Paul, 1955), 42.

November 10
Blessed William Joseph Chaminade, *Marian Writings. Vol. 1*. ed. J.B. Armbruster, SM (Dayton, Ohio: Marianist Press, 1980), 227.

November 11
Catechism of the Catholic Church, par. 1014.

November 12
St. Peter Julian Eymard, as quoted in Rosalie Marie Levy, *Joseph, the Just Man*. (Derby, New York: Daughters of St. Paul, 1955), 150.

November 13
Pope Leo XIII, as quoted in Larry Toschi, OSJ, *Husband, Father, Worker: Questions and Answers about St. Joseph*. (Liguori, MO: Liguori, 2012), 107.

November 14
Pope Leo XIII, *Quamquam Pluries,* 3.

November 15
St. Albert the Great, as quoted in Francis L. Filas, SJ, *Joseph and Jesus: A Theological Study of Their Relationship.* (Milwaukee: Bruce Publishing Co.), 62.

November 16
St. Gertrude the Great, as quoted in *Favorite Prayers to St. Joseph.* (Charlotte, North Carolina: TAN Books, 1997), 52.

November 17
Blessed Pope Pius IX, as quoted in Rev. Nicholas O'Rafferty, *Discourses on St. Joseph.* (Milwaukee: Bruce Publishing Co., 1951), 212.

November 18
Blessed Gabriele Allegra, *Mary's Immaculate Heart: A Way to God.* (Chicago, Illinois: Franciscan Herald Press, 1983), 55.

November 19
St. Teresa of Avila, as quoted in Rosalie Marie Levy, *Joseph, the Just Man.* (Derby, New York: Daughters of St. Paul, 1955), 146.

November 20
St. Lawrence of Brindisi, *Opera Omnia: Feastday Sermons.* trans. Vernon Wagner, OFM Cap (Delhi, India: Media House, 2007), 538.

November 21
Blessed William Joseph Chaminade, *Marian Writings. Vol. 1.* ed. J.B. Armbruster, SM (Dayton, Ohio: Marianist Press, 1980), 235.

November 22
St. Peter Julian Eymard, *Month of St. Joseph.* (Cleveland, Ohio: Emmanuel Publications, 1948), 101.

November 23
Blessed William Joseph Chaminade, *Marian Writings. Vol. 1.* ed. J.B. Armbruster, SM (Dayton, Ohio: Marianist Press, 1980), 229.

November 24
Pope Pius XI, as quoted in Francis L. Filas, SJ, *St. Joseph & Daily Christian Living.* (New York: Macmillan Co., 1959), 195.

November 25
Blessed William Joseph Chaminade, as quoted in *From a Full Heart: Thoughts from Father Chaminade.* (North American Center for Marianist Studies, NACMS).

Compiled by Francis J. Greiner, SM, (St. Meinard, Indiana: The Grail Press, 1949), entry for March 12.

November 26
Blessed James Alberione, *Mary, Queen of Apostles* (Boston, Massachusetts: Daughters of St. Paul, 1976), 142.

November 27
St. Leonard of Port Maurice, as quoted in Andrew Doze, *Saint Joseph: Shadow of the Father*. trans. Florestine Audett, RJM (Staten Island, New York: Alba House, 1992), 18-19.

November 28
Blessed William Joseph Chaminade, *Marian Writings. Vol. 1*. ed. J.B. Armbruster, SM (Dayton, Ohio: Marianist Press, 1980), 230.

November 29
St. Joseph Marello, as quoted in Larry Toschi, OSJ, *St. Joseph in the Lives of Two Blesseds of the Church: Blessed Junipero Serra and Blessed Joseph Marello*. (Santa Cruz, California: Guardian of the Redeemer Books, 1994), 75.

November 30
Blessed Pope Paul VI, *Homily for the Feast of St. Joseph* (March 27, 1969). www.osjusa.org

December
Image: *The Holy Family* (c.1660)
Bartolome Esteban Murillo (1617-1682)

December 1
Pope Pius XI, as quoted in Francis L. Filas, SJ, *St. Joseph & Daily Christian Living*. (New York: Macmillan Co., 1959), 195.

December 2
Blessed Pope Paul VI, *Discourse* (March 19, 1969): *Insegnamenti*, VII (1969), p. 1269.

December 3
St. Lawrence of Brindisi, *Opera Omnia: Feastday Sermons*. trans. Vernon Wagner, OFM Cap (Delhi, India: Media House, 2007), 539.

December 4
Pope Francis, *Meeting with Families in Manila, Philippines* (January 16, 2015).

December 5
St. Peter Julian Eymard, *Month of St. Joseph.* (Cleveland, Ohio: Emmanuel Publications, 1948), 41.

December 6
Pope Leo XIII, as quoted in Rosalie Marie Levy, *Joseph the Just Man.* (Derby, New York: Daughters of St. Paul, 1955), 74.

December 7
Pope Benedict XV, as quoted in Domenic de Domenico, OP, *True Devotion to St. Joseph and the Church.* (New Hope, Kentucky: New Hope Publications, 2003), 37.

December 8
Ven. Fulton J. Sheen, *The World's First Love: Mary, Mother of God.* (San Francisco: Ignatius Press, 1996), 66.

December 9
Pope Leo XIII, as quoted in Larry Toschi, OSJ, *Husband, Father, Worker: Questions and Answers about St. Joseph.* (Liguori, Missouri: Liguori, 2012), 107.

December 10
Blessed Gabriele Allegra, *Mary's Immaculate Heart: A Way to God.* (Chicago, Illinois: Franciscan Herald Press, 1983), 55.

December 11
Servant of God John A. Hardon, *St. Joseph: Foster Father of Jesus,* as quoted on www.therealpresence.org

December 12
Blessed William Joseph Chaminade, *Marian Writings. Vol. II.* ed. J.B. Armbruster, SM (Dayton, Ohio: Marianist Press, 1980), 158.

December 13
St. Josemaria Escriva, "A Homily: In Joseph's Workshop," as quoted in Michael D. Griffin, OCD, (ed), *Saint Joseph and the Third Millennium* (Hubertus, Wisconsin: Teresian Charism Press, 1999), 356.

December 14
St. John Neumann, as quoted in Joseph F. Chorpenning, OSFS, "St. Joseph's Presence in the Life and Ministry of John N. Neumann, CSsR" in *St. Joseph Studies: Papers in English from the Seventh and Eighth International St. Joseph Symposia: Malta 1997 and El Salvador 2001.* ed. Larry Toschi, OSJ (Santa Cruz, California: Guardian of the Redeemer Books, 2002), 132.

December 15

Pope Leo XIII, as quoted in Rev. Nicholas O'Rafferty, *Discourses on St. Joseph*. (Milwaukee: Bruce Publishing Co., 1951), 235-236.

December 16

Pope Benedict XVI, as quoted in Fr. Richard W. Gilsdorf, *Go to Joseph*. (Green Bay, Wisconsin: Star of the Bay Press, 2009), 124.

December 17

St. Bede the Venerable, as quoted in Florent Raymond Bilodeau, "The Virginity of Saint Joseph in the Latin Fathers and Medieval Ecclesiastical Writers," STL Dissertation. (Baltimore, Maryland: St Mary's University, 1957). Available at www.osjusa.org

December 18

St. Francis de Sales, as quoted in Fr. Marie-Dominique Philippe, OP, *The Mystery of Joseph*. (Bethesda, Maryland: Zaccheus Press, 2009), 153.

December 19

Blessed William Joseph Chaminade, *The Chaminade Legacy*. Monograph Series. Document no. 53, Volume 2. trans. Joseph Stefanelli, SM (Dayton, Ohio: NACMS, 2008), 411.

December 20

St. Francis de Sales, as quoted in Rev. Nicholas O'Rafferty, *Discourses on St. Joseph*. (Milwaukee: Bruce Publishing Co., 1951), 207.

December 21

St. Peter Julian Eymard, *Month of St. Joseph*. (Cleveland, Ohio: Emmanuel Publications, 1948), 6-7.

December 22

St. Stanislaus Papczynski, *St. Stanislaus Papczynski: The Life and Writings of the Marians' Founder*. (Stockbridge, Massachusetts: Marian Press, 2016), 87.

December 23

Catechism of the Catholic Church, par. 1846.

December 24

Blessed John Henry Newman, as quoted in Maria Cecilia Baij, OSB, *The Life of St. Joseph*. (Asbury, New Jersey: 101 Foundation, Inc., 1996), 422.

December 25

Blessed William Joseph Chaminade, *Marian Writings. Vol. 1*. ed. J.B. Armbruster, SM (Dayton, Ohio: Marianist Press, 1980), 235.

December 26
St. Francis de Sales, as quoted in Rosalie Marie Levy, *Joseph the Just Man*. (Derby, New York: Daughters of St. Paul, 1955), 130.

December 27
Catechism of the Catholic Church, par. 437.

December 28
Pope Benedict XV, *Bonum Sane,* as quoted in Francis L. Filas, SJ, *St. Joseph & Daily Christian Living*. (New York: Macmillan Co., 1959), 192.

December 29
St. Peter Julian Eymard, *Month of St. Joseph*. (Cleveland, Ohio: Emmanuel Publications, 1948), 94.

December 30
Pope Benedict XV, *Bonum Sane,* as quoted in Francis L. Filas, SJ, *St. Joseph & Daily Christian Living*. (New York: Macmillan Co., 1959), 192.

December 31
St. John Paul II, *Redemptoris Custos*, 32.

Reflections

About the Author

Father Donald Calloway, MIC, a convert to Catholicism, is a member of the Congregation of Marian Fathers of the Immaculate Conception. Before his conversion, he was a high school dropout who had been kicked out of a foreign country, institutionalized twice, and thrown in jail multiple times. After his radical conversion, he earned a BA in philosophy and theology from the Franciscan University of Steubenville, MDiv and STB degrees from the Dominican House of Studies in Washington, D.C., and an STL in Mariology from the International Marian Research Institute in Dayton, Ohio. In addition to *St. Joseph Gems: Daily Wisdom on our Spiritual Father*, he has also written *26 Champions of the Rosary* (Marian Press, 2017), *How to Pray the Rosary* (Marian Press, 2017), the best-selling books *Champions of the Rosary: The History and Heroes of a Spiritual Weapon* (Marian Press, 2016); *Under the Mantle: Marian Thoughts from a 21ˢᵗ Century Priest* (Marian Press, 2013); and *No Turning Back: A Witness to Mercy* (Marian Press, 2010), a bestseller that recounts his dramatic conversion story. He also is the author of the book *Purest of All Lilies: The Virgin Mary in the Spirituality of St. Faustina* (Marian Press, 2008). He introduced and arranged *Marian Gems: Daily Wisdom on Our Lady* (Marian Press, 2014) and *Rosary Gems: Daily Wisdom on the Holy Rosary* (Marian Press, 2015). Further, he has written many academic articles and is the editor of two books: *The Immaculate Conception in the Life of the Church* (Marian Press, 2004) and *The Virgin Mary and Theology of the Body* (Marian Press, 2005).

Father Calloway is the vicar provincial and vocation director for the Mother of Mercy Province.

Marian Inspiration from Fr. Calloway

Y74-MGEM

Marian Gems
Daily Wisdom on Our Lady

In *Marian Gems: Daily Wisdom on Our Lady*, Fr. Donald Calloway, MIC, shares gems or quotes on Mary. He includes a gem for each day of the year, drawn from the writings of the popes, saints, blesseds, and venerables. When these gems first appeared in his book *Under the Mantle*, many readers loved them and suggested he publish them in a separate book for daily prayer. Paperback. 232 pages.

Rosary Gems
Daily Wisdom on the Holy Rosary

Inspired by his own love for the Rosary and the saints, Fr. Donald Calloway, MIC, has gathered and arranged into one book one of the largest collections of quotes on the Rosary to ever appear in print. The quotes have been selected from the writings of popes, saints, blesseds, and the many venerables of the Church. This is the perfect book to help you rediscover the power and wisdom of the holy Rosary! Paperback, 245 pages. Y74-RGEM

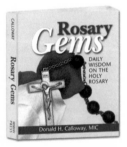

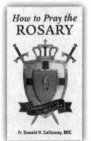

How to Pray the Rosary

In this handy little guide, best-selling author Fr. Donald Calloway, MIC, teaches you how to pray the Rosary well and why it matters, addressing issues such as:

- Why pray the Rosary?
- How long should a well-prayed Rosary take?
- What are the graces attached to praying the Rosary?
- How can I become a champion of the Rosary?

Our Lady needs Rosary champions to help bring peace in the world. Will you answer her call to prayer? Y74-HPR *ebook*: Y74-EBHPR

Call 1-800-462-7426 or visit www.fathercalloway.com

Marian Inspiration from Fr. Calloway

Champions of the Rosary:
The History and Heroes of a Spiritual Weapon

Champions of the Rosary, by best-selling author Fr. Donald Calloway, MIC, tells the powerful story of the history of the Rosary and the champions of this devotion. The Rosary is a spiritual sword with the power to conquer sin, defeat evil, and bring about peace. Read this book to deepen your understanding of and love for praying the Rosary. Endorsed by 30 bishops from around the world! Paperback, 428 pages. Y74-CRBK

Thirteenth of the Month Club

**Father Donald Calloway, MIC,
Marian vocation director,
participates in a recurring feature in the
Thirteenth of the Month Club newsletter.**

I'm honored and delighted to do this for the club, since it's a good way for me to help people come to a better place in their relationship with Our Lady. I want to let people know that by being in the Thirteenth of the Month Club, they're part of the Marian family. They are praying for us [the Marian Fathers of the Immaculate Conception], and we are praying for them.

Thirteenth of the Month Club members are a group of special friends who help support the work of the Marian Fathers of the Immaculate Conception. On the 13th of each month, members pray the Rosary for the intentions of the Club. The Marians residing in Fatima offer a special Mass on the 13th of the month for members' intentions. All members pledge a monthly gift and receive the Club newsletter, published by the Association of Marian Helpers, Stockbridge, MA 01263.

For more information, call: 1-413-298-1382
Online: marian.org/13th   E-mail: thirteenth@marian.org

The Marian Fathers of today and tomorrow

What are you looking for in the priests of tomorrow?

- ✓ Zeal for proclaiming the Gospel
- ✓ Faithfulness to the Pope and Church teaching
- ✓ Love of Mary Immaculate
- ✓ Love of the Holy Eucharist
- ✓ Concern for the souls in Purgatory
- ✓ Dedication to bringing God's mercy to all souls

These are the top reasons why men pursuing a priestly vocation are attracted to the Congregation of Marian Fathers of the Immaculate Conception.

Please support the education of these future priests. Nearly 150 Marian seminarians are counting on your gift.

1-413-298-1382   marian.org/helpseminarians

Join the
Association of Marian Helpers,
headquartered at the National Shrine of The Divine Mercy, and share in special blessings!

**An invitation from
Fr. Joseph, MIC, the director**

Marian Helpers is an Association of Christian faithful of the Congregation of Marian Fathers of the Immaculate Conception.

By becoming a member, you share in the spiritual benefits of the daily Masses, prayers, and good works of the Marian priests and brothers. This is a special offer of grace given to you by the Church through the Marian Fathers.

Please consider this opportunity to share in these blessings, along with others whom you would wish to join into this spiritual communion.

Call 1-800-462-7426 or visit marian.org

Enroll Loved Ones

Give a Consoling Gift: *Prayer*

Enroll your loved ones in the Association of Marian Helpers, and they will be remembered in the daily Masses, prayers, good works, and merits of the Marian priests and brothers around the world.

Request a Mass

to be offered by the Marian Fathers for your loved one:

Individual Masses (for the living or deceased)
Gregorian Masses (30 days of consecutive Masses for the deceased)

1-800-462-7426
marian.org/enrollments   **marian.org/mass**